Testing to Learn—
Learning to Test

Joanne Capper

International Reading Association
800 Barksdale Road, PO Box 8139
Newark, Delaware 19714-8139, USA

AED·

Academy for Educational Development
1875 Connecticut Avenue, NW
Washington, DC 20009-1202, USA

The International Reading Association attempts, through its publications, to provide a forum for a wide spectrum of opinions on reading. This policy permits divergent viewpoints without implying the endorsement of the Association.

Director of Publications   Joan M. Irwin
Assistant Director of Publications   Wendy Lapham Russ
Senior Editor   Christian A. Kempers
Associate Editor   Matthew W. Baker
Assistant Editor   Janet S. Parrack
Editorial Assistant   Cynthia C. Sawaya
Association Editor   David K. Roberts
Production Department Manager   Iona Sauscermen
Graphic Design Coordinator   Boni Nash
Design Consultant   Larry F. Husfelt
Electronic Publishing Supervisor   Wendy A. Mazur
Electronic Publishing Specialist   Anette Schütz-Ruff
Electronic Publishing Specialist   Cheryl J. Strum

Cover Photograph   © Sonjai A. Reynolds. Used by permission.

Copyright 1996 by the International Reading Association and the Academy for Educational Development.

Materials contained in this publication were originally developed by the Academy for Educational Development, Washington, DC, under the Advancing Basic Education and Literacy Project (ABEL 1) for the United States Agency for International Development (USAID).

This work is a derivative work based on materials developed under USAID Contract No. DPE-5832-Z-00-9032-00.

Library of Congress Cataloging-in-Publication Data
Capper, Joanne
    Testing to learn—learning to test/Joanne Capper.
        p.   cm.
    Includes bibliographical references and indexes.
    1. Educational tests and measurements   2. Academic achievement—Testing.
3. Learning—Evaluation.   4. Educational evaluation—Planning.   I. Title.
LB3051.C347   1996   96-32876
371.2'6—dc20
ISBN 0-87207-145-6 (pbk. : alk. paper)

CONTENTS

FOREWORD

Testing to Learn—Learning to Test was written in response to a growing recognition, in both developed and developing countries, that what is tested is what is taught in schools. Testing has assumed increasing importance worldwide because education has become the preeminent means for social mobility, an engine for economic growth, and the mechanism for inculcating a sense of national unity. Testing, as the "gateway" mechanism for students, and as a means for monitoring educational quality and efficiency of a nation's schools, has increased in importance as education competes with other sectors for scarce public resources.

This book and the companion summary describe how examinations and national assessments can be used to encourage more pedagogically sound teaching and learning. Based on recent research and classroom experience, Testing to Learn—Learning to Test provides concrete examples of ways to measure student learning and describes how to develop, score, and interpret tests to ensure that they are valid, reliable, and fair to all children. It offers techniques and guidelines to increase the involvement of parents, teachers, and students in the use of tests to motivate and improve the educational system—not just judge it. These examples and guidelines are offered to educational policymakers, recognizing the many constraints within which educational systems in developing countries must operate.

Although the primary focus of the book is on formal systems of schooling, the discussions and examples, particularly those related to classroom-level testing and teacher training, are equally applicable to nonformal activities.

We hope that this work will reawaken educational policymakers to the importance of testing and will prompt a thoughtful reassessment of examinations and the contribution that national assessment systems can make to promoting educational quality. We hope that from this assessment will emerge new approaches to the involvement of government, parents, teachers, and students in education and its consequences.

Kurt D. Moses
Vice President
Academy for Educational Development

ACKNOWLEDGMENTS

Testing to Learn—Learning to Test describes a new view of the role of examinations and national assessments in relation to the central acts of education—teaching and learning. It is based on dramatic changes occurring worldwide in the design and use of testing systems and addresses the technical, social, pedagogical, and policy dimensions of the interaction between testing and teaching. The writing of this publication represents one facet of the Project ABEL (Advancing Basic Education and Literacy) mandate to describe activities that work in the improvement of basic education throughout the world.

This book was begun as an applied research effort under the USAID/Research and Development/Education Office–funded Project ABEL. Under the general project oversight of James Hoxeng, Project ABEL, through the Academy for Educational Development, supported the development of this book and companion summary to highlight concrete experiences and actual practices that could improve testing systems throughout the developing world. A preliminary version of the summary was supported by USAID/Pakistan under the Primary Education Development (PED) Program.

A number of people contributed to this effort. Kurt Moses, Vice President, Academy for Educational Development, was responsible for obtaining support for the publication and offered extensive editorial advice. Significant contributions to the conceptual development of the text have been made by a number of U.S. and international testing experts and policymakers, including Ben Makau of Research and Evaluation Associates, Kenya; Peliwe Lolwana of the Independent Examinations Board, South Africa; Anthony Somerset of the United Kingdom; Fuad Abou Hatab of the National Council for Educational Examinations and Evaluation, Egypt; David Ongom and Cyprian Cele of the Uganda National Examinations Board, Uganda; the late Sar Biland Khan of the Ontario Institute for Studies in Education, Canada; W. James Popham of IOX Assessment Associates, United States; Anthony Nitko of the University of Pittsburgh, United States; David Carroll of the United Kingdom; Karma El-Hassan of the American University of Beirut, Lebanon; Ype H. Poortinga of Tilburg University, The Netherlands; Ash Hartwell of USAID, Africa Bureau, Washington, DC; Annie Myeni of the United Nations, New York; Mary Rauner of USAID, Washington, DC; and Marolyn Hatch of Virginia. Sarah B. Alturki, of Saudi Arabia, provided for the translation and printing of an Arabic version of the Executive Summary. Editorial and technical writing assistance at AED was provided by Sonjai Reynolds, Barbara O'Grady, Francy Hays, and John Hatch.

I trust that this work will contribute to the dialogue about reforming examinations and designing national assessments in the service of high-quality teaching and learning.

TESTING TERMINOLOGY

Assessment	A process for obtaining information that is used for making decisions about students, curricula and programs, and educational policy.
Assessment techniques	Includes formal and informal observations of students, paper-and-pencil tests, student homework and research papers, project performances, oral questioning, analyses of students' records, and lab work.
Criterion-referenced tests	Tests developed to determine whether an individual has learned specific skills or knowledge.
Evaluation	The process of making a value judgment about the worth of someone or something. May or may not be based on measurements or test results.
Grade/class/standard	Terms used to indicate a specific academic year in the schooling progression, such as grade 3, class 3, or standard 3. The term "grade" is commonly used in the United States; the terms "class" and "standard" are used in English-speaking African countries and other former British colonies. "Standard" is generally used to denote a specific year of schooling at the primary, or elementary, level; "form" denotes a specific year at the secondary level, beginning with form 1 for the 9th year of school and ending with form 4 for the 12th year of school.
Item	A test question.
Mark/score/grade	Terms used to indicate assigning a score to a paper, report, or test based on predetermined criteria. The term "mark" is more common in English-speaking African countries; the terms "score" and "grade" are used frequently in the United States.
Measurement	A procedure for assigning numbers (usually called scores) to a specified attribute or characteristic of persons in such a way that the numbers describe the degree to which the persons possess the attribute.
National assessment	A national government's systematic efforts to collect, report, and use information about the status and progress of its educational system, including student achievement. Data generally is collected on a sample of students and reported at the school, district, provincial, or regional levels, but seldom at the student level. In

some countries, assessments are conducted at the state or provincial levels.

Norm-referenced tests   Tests designed to compare student performance with a norm group of students, rather than to determine how proficient a student is in a particular subject, skill, or concept.

Reliability   The extent to which a test yields the same results on repeated administrations, or the extent to which different raters assign the same score to a student's performance on a test or task.

Tests   Instruments or systematic procedures for observing and describing one or more characteristics of a student using either a numerical scale or classification scheme. Also referred to as examinations in some countries. Examinations refer to tests used to (1) certify that a student has learned what was taught during that cycle, (2) determine if the student has learned enough to justify promotion to the next level, or (3) select students for a limited number of places at the next level of schooling.

Tests can provide information about an individual or a system. They can be used to determine whether school systems have attained certain goals. When used to describe systems, the score is usually the average score of the pupils who took the test in a school, district, region, or state.

Validity   The extent to which a test measures what is purports to measure. Validity is concerned with the interpretations and decisions made that are based on the test results.

INTRODUCTION
Using Testing as a Policy Tool

Educational policymakers can use tests as a policy tool to improve teaching and learning. Both examinations and national assessments can be designed to convey powerful messages to teachers, parents, and students about what knowledge and skills are important to learn and the way they should be taught. This book conveys ways testing can be used as a powerful and cost-effective policy tool to improve educational quality. The technical and policy aspects of educational testing,[1] along with the steps needed to use testing to influence better teaching and learning, will be explained.

Tests have an impact on what is taught and learned in classrooms, especially when the results of the tests are used to make important decisions (such as granting certification to graduating students, promoting students to higher grades, or selecting students for higher levels of education). Evidence has shown that teachers and students devote great amounts of time to teaching and learning those topics they expect will be on a test. One study found that time spent preparing for and recovering from tests amounted to 100 hours of instructional time per year (Smith, 1991). Many countries complain that their education system is so exam ridden that the entire teaching and learning process is geared to passing the exam and

getting the good marks needed for entry to higher levels of education. Another study (Rowell & Prophet, 1990), involving science instruction, reported the following:

> In the observed classrooms, completion of the worksheets with the "correct" answer has become the goal of every science lesson despite a postulated student-centered inquiry approach. The race against time required to complete all the worksheets prior to the government examination has led to considerable cutting of the hands-on activities.... (p. 20)

The higher the stakes associated with tests, the more time and attention will be devoted to preparing for them.[2] If the tests do not measure important and meaningful content, skills, and knowledge, then precious time and resources are wasted.

Until recently, educators had not realized how powerful the influence of tests is on teaching and learning. After years of testing throughout the world, it has become increasingly apparent that what is tested is what gets taught and *how* something is tested influences *how* it gets taught and learned. For example, if a test focuses solely on factual knowledge, teachers will teach factual knowledge; if a test focuses on reasoning, analysis, and solving real-life problems, teachers are more likely to teach students to reason, analyze, and solve problems.

Educators and test developers around the world are beginning to consider seriously the power that tests have and the way in which they influence teaching and learning. They are redesigning tests and testing systems to reflect, guide, and influence teaching and learning in ways that are consistent with research findings about effective learning and with revised views of what educators think that students should be learning.

Testing is an opportunity to redirect the focus of education to its essence—good teaching and learning. A well-designed testing system offers policymakers repeated opportunities to focus attention on what should be learned, why it is important to be learned, how it should be learned, and how learning can be improved. If implemented properly, a well-designed testing system can be one of the most powerful points of leverage a policymaker has to improve the quality of education in a nation's schools.

Testing can make the intellectual essence of schooling explicit. Textbooks and curricula articulate this essence, but when they are placed in schools and classrooms, the public dialogue becomes muted—narrowed to only those who participate in the day-to-day events of classrooms and schools. Testing can be used to engage and inform educators and the public about better teaching and learning—about what it means to think, to understand, and to solve real problems. It can help transform conceptions of schooling beyond basic skills and rote memorization and promote more intellectually rich and emotionally invigorating classrooms.

What does this mean for educational policymakers and others involved in developing tests? A poorly designed testing system can hinder the most dedicated efforts to improve instructional quality, but a well-designed system can become a spearhead for educational improvement. Policymakers can harness the power of testing in order to contribute to better education for all students. Effective use of this power requires

- time to understand the principles of good teaching and learning that have become more explicit because of recent research on learning;
- time to understand the technical and policy aspects of testing; and
- a commitment to ensure that certain critical steps are taken to design and use a technically accurate, educationally sound, and intellectually consistent testing program.

This book is intended to help educational policymakers, planners, and measurement specialists in developing countries strengthen the capacity of their testing system to contribute to national development. It provides the information needed to evaluate and improve testing systems in a way that will contribute to better teaching and learning. It addresses the policy, technical, and public relations aspects of the testing process. Although testing typically is viewed as a technical activity, it is also an instrument of social control, especially in developing countries. Entire families' lives can be influenced by a child's performance on an examination because that performance can constrain or expand future employment possibilities for the child. Because of this powerful social influence, parents, teachers, and students often are concerned when changes are made to examinations; even though they may resent current examinations, they will likely view changes as a threat. For this reason, this book addresses the social dimensions of testing reform and each component of the testing reform process.

Chapter 1 contains an overview of key principles of good teaching and learning that should be considered when developing and analyzing tests. Chapter 2 outlines the differences between examinations and assessments and suggests ways policymakers can use each to improve educational quality. Differences between norm- and criterion-referenced tests are discussed, and continuous assessment is defined. Chapter 3 explains different types of test items and the ways each type may influence teaching and learning. Chapter 4 discusses the importance of creating specifications and marking guides to improve essay tests, of conducting marking sessions in groups, and of providing training to those who will mark essay tests. Chapter 5 suggests ways that examinations, national assessments, and continuous assessment can be integrated. Chapter 6 discusses the importance of preparing a test plan that provides an opportunity for relevant groups and individuals to consider what is most important for students to know and do. Chapter 7 details item specifications: what they are, why they are important, and what they look like. Chapter 8 addresses ways test results can be used to help improve teachers' classroom practice and to provide useful information to policymakers. And, finally, Chapter 9 of-

fers a summary of the steps needed to improve a testing system so that it has a positive influence on teaching and learning; it also highlights some potential difficulties to avoid when preparing a testing system.

The appendixes provide examples of various aspects of an effective testing system, such as sample performance tasks, open-ended questions, marking guides, and test-item specifications.

Notes

[1]The term "test" or "testing" is used to refer to both examinations and assessments. When referring only to examinations, the term "examination" or "exam" will be used; when referring to assessments, the term "assessment" or "national assessment" will be used. Please refer to Chapter 2 for a more complete description of examinations, assessments, and tests.

[2]High-stakes tests are ones that have major consequences, such as promotion, selection, or scholarships; low-stakes tests have minor consequences. National assessments are considered to be low stakes because they generally measure achievement on a sampling basis rather than achievement of individual students.

CHAPTER 1

Principles of Good Teaching and Learning: Implications for Testing

Numerous studies have shown that much of the learning that occurs in classrooms around the world is superficial learning. Facts, rules, and formulas are memorized, but often this information is not connected in a coherent framework that would allow students to make sense of it and to use it in new situations. Remembering and using knowledge are the essence of education. It is a waste of time and scarce resources to teach students facts or skills that they are unable to access and use when appropriate. Instruction that relies primarily on teaching children to acquire facts and neglects teaching them the relations among and use of those facts fails to impart real understanding. Such learning is viewed by students and teachers as getting through the textbook and passing the test rather than understanding and using the acquired knowledge.

Tests may contribute to this superficial learning and may give inaccurate impressions of how well something has been learned. This happens when a test comprises questions that simply require that students recall facts. For example, students may be able to respond correctly to tests that contain questions such as, "What was the most important discovery that marked the beginning of the New Stone Age?" or "In which African country was writing on papyrus practiced?" Some of this type of knowledge is important for students to learn, but when a test relies primarily on factual questions, teachers often do not encourage students to understand the significance, meaning, or use of such knowledge. Factual recall questions do not require that students apply their knowledge, demonstrate how one piece of knowledge is connected to another, or see the patterns and relations among various pieces of knowledge that combine to form concepts—the basis for knowing, thinking, and doing.

Children do not attend school simply to acquire facts; they go to school to learn to think and to solve the numerous academic and real-life problems they will encounter throughout their personal and professional lives. No school can teach students everything they need to know, especially with the rapid growth in information proliferated by computers and modern forms of information transmission. Schooling offers children the information, concepts, and intellectual skills needed to apply to the more complex questions they will encounter throughout their lives. Schooling should enable individuals to become independent thinkers and to solve problems.

Evidence suggests that school systems sometimes incorporate procedures and systems that promote superficial learning and undermine more meaningful, in-depth learning. A curriculum that is overburdened with too many subjects and topics, textbooks that cover topics superficially, and tests that measure and reinforce rote memorization undermine meaningful learning. Confronted with such requirements, even the most dedicated and capable teachers are forced to teach subjects superficially. Under these conditions, teachers' measure of success is to cover the material in the curriculum and textbook and make sure that students pass the test. Teachers have little time to ensure that students understand and apply what they are learning, especially if this learning is not what is measured on the tests. Redesigning tests to measure deep-level understanding, higher order thinking, and the application of learning to real-life situations can help promote changes in classrooms.

The next section is a review of the basic principles of instruction that foster meaningful and useful teaching and learning in which students think, reflect, and solve an array of academic and real-life problems. The basic principles are (1) cover important topics in depth, (2) make instruction coherent, (3) promote active learning, (4) use real-life tasks, (5) make students aware of their learning, and (6) teach students to manage their learning. Each of these principles must be structured into the curricula, textbooks, and instruction before better testing systems can be implemented. A pedagogically sound curriculum is necessary for good teaching and learning. An excellent test cannot make up for or countermand an overburdened curriculum or text-

book. The link among curricula, textbooks, teaching, learning, and testing is essential and is emphasized throughout this book. The review of the teaching principles is followed by examples of several test items and performance tasks that illustrate the application of the principles in a testing context.

Before a review of the basic principles of teaching, a brief discussion of higher order thinking is offered because it is a primary goal of schooling and underlies these principles.

Higher Order Thinking

Many educators often are unclear about the definition of higher order thinking and what it means for developing curricula, textbooks, teacher training, and tests. A common representation of higher order thinking is Bloom's (1956) Taxonomy of Educational Objectives, but this listing and defining of thinking skills has obscured the more subtle nature of thinking. Resnick (1987, p. 3) has articulated higher order thinking in more detail. Her description may be useful when developing tests that measure higher order thinking and may help clarify the principles of good teaching and learning described later. Higher order thinking

- is nonalgorithmic—that is, the path of action is not fully specified in advance.
- tends to be complex; the total solution path is not apparent from any single vantage point.
- often results in multiple solutions, each with costs and benefits, rather than a single, best solution.
- requires subtle judgments and interpretations.

- involves uncertainty; not everything involved in the task is known.

- involves managing one's own thinking processes; higher order thinking is not likely to occur when students are told what to do at every step.

- requires effort.

Higher order thinking is the type of thinking people do every day. Students who develop higher level thinking skills will be prepared to function more effectively outside of school. However, most classroom teaching seldom offers students opportunities to engage in higher order thinking. Instead, answers are either right or wrong, a question usually has only one right answer, students are not asked to make subtle judgments or interpretations, problems are seldom complex, and students are usually told precisely what to do. Rowell and Prophet (1990, p. 19) observed the following dialogue in a science lesson. It is an example of a lesson that requires little or no higher order thinking of students, and yet it is typical of classroom dialogues worldwide.

Teacher:	Now let's go back to solutions and so on. I heat water in a basin, and it eventually disappears. Where does it go?
Student:	It evaporates.
Teacher:	In the form of?
Student:	The form of gas.
Teacher:	I want the name.
Student:	Steam.
Teacher:	Why steam, not water vapor?
Student:	Because it is hot.
Teacher:	What is a solute?

Student:	Salty water.
Teacher:	No, salty water is a solution.
Student:	The solute is the salt.
Teacher:	And the solvent is the liquid. What can you do to collect evaporating water?

The researcher who observed this classroom interaction commented,

The notable features of these exchanges are the brevity of the required responses and the low level of cognitive functioning demanded of the student by the teacher. The teacher appears satisfied with simple recall of terms, allowing students to be completely detached from the meanings. (p. 20)

The researcher also reported that the teacher gave students a complete set of notes to prepare them for the examinations. The teacher offered the following justification for her behavior:

I think the students prefer to have the worksheets because they [the sheets] pick out all the main points from the textbook. Students do not like having to make notes from the text. (p. 20)

Rowell and Prophet (1990) argue that teacher-prepared test notes eliminate opportunities for students to develop their analytical skills. Being able to distinguish what is important within a body of knowledge is essential to understanding and using knowledge.

Figure 1 contains a set of test questions designed to engage secondary students in higher levels of thinking. The questions involve subtle judgments and interpretations, are complex, require effort, require that students manage their thinking processes, and engage

FIGURE 1

Example of Test Questions Promoting Higher Levels of Thinking

Final Votes for Each Party in African Election

The National Assembly

Party	Seats	Percentage	Votes
African National Congress	252	62.7%	2,256,824
National Party	82	20.4%	3,983,690
Inkatha Freedom Party	43	10.5%	2,058,294
Freedom Front	9	2.2%	424,555
Democratic Party	7	1.7%	338,426
Pan African Congress	5	1.2%	243,478
Minor Parties			
SP		0.1%	10,575
KISS		0%	5,916
WRPP		0%	6,434
WLP		0%	4,159
XPP		0%	6,320
AMP		0.2%	34,466
ACDP	2	0.5%	88,104
ADM		0.1%	9,886
AMCP		0.1%	27,690
DPSA		0.1%	19,451
FP		0.1%	17,663
LSAP		0%	3,293
MFP		0.1%	13,433

The final count

■ **Votes counted: 19,726,579**
■ **Accepted: 19,533,498**
■ **Spoilt: 193,081**

Full names of smaller parties; ■ **SP:** Sports Organisation for Collective Contributions and Equal Rights ■ **Kiss:** Keep It Straight and Simple Party ■ **WRPP:** Women's Rights Peace Party ■ **WLP:** Workers' List Party ■ **XPP:** Ximoko Progressive Party ■ **AMP:** Africa Muslim Party ■ **ACDP:** African Christian Democratic Party ■ **ADM:** African Democratic Movement ■ **AMCP:** African Moderates Congress Party ■ **DPSA:** Dikwankwetla Party of SA ■ **FP:** Federal Party ■ **LSAP:** Luso-South African Party ■ **MFP:** Minority Front Party

1. Write a short paragraph on what the information in the chart reveals.

2. An error has been made in writing that the number of African National Congress votes is 2,256,824. Since we know the ANC received 62.7% of the votes, work out as accurately as possible how many votes the ANC actually received.

3. A party receives a seat in the national assembly for every 25% of the votes. Show that this is true using the data in the chart.

4. How many more votes did the ACDP get than the MFP?

Adapted from *The Mathematics Assessment Package* (Adult Basic Education, Level 3, User Guide 2), produced by the Independent Examinations Board, 1994, Johannesburg, South Africa.

students in analytical skills that are directly relevant to their lives. This set of questions, which refers to the accompanying table, is designed to measure the following objective: Describe and interpret information from tables, bar graphs, pie charts, line graphs, and pictograms.

Students of *all* ages and abilities are capable of thinking and solving problems and should be given opportunities to engage in higher order thinking and to solve interesting problems. Higher order thinking requires that students have sufficient time to think about and do assignments rather than be told that all tasks must be done under a tight deadline. Students also should have opportunities to rethink and revise their work.

The science lesson dialogue given earlier is cited not because it is unique but because it is so common. Higher order thinking is not well understood nor are the instructional approaches a teacher might use to promote such thinking. Educators are beginning to realize that tests can be developed to make explicit what higher order thinking is and how to teach it in the classroom.

This does not mean that only higher order skills should be taught or tested. What is taught or tested depends on a nation's goals and objectives, which are likely to require a combination of cognitive levels. Many lower order objectives are an essential part of any curriculum. However, in this book, the emphasis is on teaching higher order thinking because it is typically neglected or poorly done.

Chapter 3 contains several exemplary test questions, or tasks, designed to encourage higher level thinking and problem solving. Many of these tasks are intellectually engaging and have a spirited, almost fun, element to them. Some educators believe that learning should not be fun—a "no pain, no gain" view of learning. However, research does not support this view as being conducive to learning; in fact, pain and stress can hinder learning (Nummela & Rosengren, 1986). The evidence suggests that when students believe that they can learn, that they will enjoy learning, and that learning will be exhilarating, they are more likely to learn more and learn faster. When students expect learning to be painful and difficult, a part of their brain puts up barriers that interfere with learning. In several countries, the common view is that learning should not be enjoyable. This view could be a major obstacle to achieving quality learning and should be addressed at the policy level and in the design of curricula, textbooks, and teacher training. If children enjoy what is happening at school, they are more likely to attend school and to complete their schooling.

Principles of Good Teaching and Learning

Principle 1: Cover Important Topics in Depth

Simply exposing students to information will not cause them to understand or use that information; instead, students must be provided with experiences that allow them to learn the knowledge at a much deeper level than is typically provided in most curricula and textbooks. Learning at a deep level requires that more time be devoted to important topics and that students be given opportunities to learn these topics in various ways.

Overburdened curricula. An overburdened curriculum leads to a fragmented curriculum and undermines in-depth learning. Often, too many topics are included in an attempt to ensure that students are exposed to those topics. This leaves little time for students to study anything in depth and, in turn, leads to superficial learning that is soon forgotten. For example, to foster rural development, practical subjects such as health, nutrition, home economics, agriculture, and prevocational skills have been added to the curricula in many countries. In addition, many curricula include instruction in the local language, in a metropolitan language, and in religion. This instruction is included to address the needs of students who will not continue to the secondary level and will likely live in rural areas, supporting themselves from agriculture or a small business.

The rationale for including many subjects is sound and defensible, but the result may be the opposite of what is intended. Some countries require as many as 12 to 14 subjects to be taught in primary school (Eisemon, 1990). With so many different subjects, students have little time to process what they learn or to connect the new information to what they already know or learn in other subjects. For example, when required to teach 12 different subjects, teachers have only about 15 to 20 minutes per subject per day after taking roll and accounting for transitions between subjects. Students are left with an intellectually unengaging and unsatisfying learning experience. They have no time to reflect, create, connect, or imagine. Such superficial learning is a major contributor to high repetition and dropout rates and to a lack of motivation.

One way to determine whether the curriculum is realistic is to ask a group of teachers to estimate how long it takes to teach each of the topics covered in the curriculum. It is important that they are asked to specify how long it takes most of their students to *learn* the topic, not only how long they allocate to teaching the topic. This would involve some discussions about the level of mastery that students need to acquire in order to be considered as having learned the topic. Sometimes topics are included for introductory purposes, in which case students' mastery of the topic would not be expected.

After these time estimates have been provided, they should be added across all topics and subjects within a grade level and subtracted from the number of hours allocated for the school year, excluding holidays and other noninstructional times. This should provide curriculum developers and other interested groups with a realistic estimate regarding the validity of a curriculum and allow them to make needed adjustments. A curriculum that is not possible for most students to learn and understand cannot be considered valid.

Overburdened textbooks. Textbooks also can contribute to superficial teaching and learning. Based on overburdened curricula, overburdened textbooks cover too many topics and often provide meager and disjointed explanations of complex ideas. For example, an analysis of a West African grade 6 mathematics textbook revealed that 126 topics were covered in the book, with approximately 1.49 topics to be covered each day (Capper, 1994). There were only an average of 1.25 pages devoted to a topic, and many of the topics were laden with unfamiliar and difficult terminology (such as rhombus, parallelogram, rational numbers, prime numbers, dividend, line segment, and factors), sometimes with several such words on a single page. Although some of these words may look familiar to students, many are likely to be only vaguely familiar and not fully understood. Such words and concepts require more time for children to process, and when teachers are compelled by the curriculum to move rapidly through the class textbook to cover all the material, they are unlikely to take the time to ensure that all students can process and understand each concept. Many students will fall further and further behind until they finally become frustrated and give up.

Superficial textbooks. A comparison of two primary-level science texts also helps illustrate the profound influence a textbook can have on the quality of teaching and learning in a classroom; it also conveys the difficulty test developers may encounter when attempting to write test items that measure higher level thinking and deep, meaningful learning based on such books. In the first science text, for grade 5 students, 16 major topics are covered, each by only 2 or 3 pages. In the second text, for grade 6 students, only 3 major topics are covered, with each presented in considerable depth.

The difference between these two texts is best illustrated by looking at how both cover the topic of "light." The first discusses this topic in a two-page chapter, and the material has little or no connection to the other 15 chapters in the text (such as water, clouds, machines, magnetism, electrostatics, structure of the earth, and oceans). None of the 16 chapters in this text covers any of the topics in depth, and students can do little more than memorize the terminology or a few phrases.

The second, more coherent text (from McClenan & Morgan, 1989) deals with fewer topics at far deeper levels, so students are much more likely to understand, remember, and use what they are learning. This text devotes almost 60 pages to the theme of light and addresses several important subtopics: field of vision; parts and function of the eye; comparison of how eyes and lenses (both camera and glasses lenses) work; sources of light; luminous and illuminated objects; the way light travels (including transparent, translucent, and opaque objects and eclipses and mirrors); the way light gives objects color; and uses of light (including the need for light for plants and animals).

Students learning about light using the first book would spend only one or two days before moving on to another of the 16 unrelated topics. Using the second book that contains 3 topics, however, students likely would spend up to one-third of the year studying light in all its many facets. These students would gain a much deeper understanding of light, experience many opportunities to engage in hands-on activities to help them see how science is studied as a discipline, have ample time to reflect on the various dimensions of light, and have the opportunity to experience the intellectual satisfaction of studying a topic in depth.

The contrast between these two primary-level science texts exemplifies what research has found that distinguishes between superficial and transient learning and lasting and useful learning. One simply skims the surface of topics, leaving teachers and students with little to do other than to memorize a collection of disjointed and unrelated facts, and the other conveys deep-level meaning and understanding.

Implications for testing. If the curriculum or textbooks cover too many topics and cover them superficially, the preferred strategy is to redesign curricula, textbooks, and tests to promote deep-level learning and real understanding of what has been learned, so that they are coherent and consistent instructional tools. A test can be redesigned to direct the instructional focus to more integrated skills and concepts and to promote analysis, reasoning, connectedness, and real-life applications.

After appropriate changes have been made in curricula, textbooks, and tests, it is important to communicate to teachers, parents, and students that fewer, theme-based topics will be tested. Teachers should be shown illustrative test items that would require that students spend more time studying a topic in a real-life, hands-on way and at greater levels of depth. (Sample test items and performance tasks are provided in Chapter 3.)

Principle 2: Make Instruction Coherent

Coherence is a critical factor in understanding and making sense of information. It is what holds bits and pieces of information or ideas together and connects new content to existing knowledge and experiences. Coherence helps students remember and understand what they learn. It may be easier to understand how powerful the concept of coherence is if the lack of coherence is considered—which is incoherence. If someone is referred to as "incoherent," it means that person does not make sense. Much of the instruction that students receive is incoherent to them—it does not make sense. They may know the bits and pieces of what they learn, but students are often unable to access and use that knowledge when appropriate (for instance, they cannot relate the fact that the earth rotates on its axis to understanding the position of the sun in the sky). If instruction does not make sense and is not coherent, students cannot remember it or use it.

Revolutionary new findings in brain research support what scientists and learning theorists have suspected for some time: the more connections a person can make in relation to a topic, the more likely that person is to remember and use that knowledge. The drawing of a section of the brain on the next page shows the pathways in the brain through which information and thoughts are transmitted. Some of the pathways are thick, and others are thin and wispy. Scientists now know that the thick pathways represent a rich and interconnected web of experience and knowledge, and the thin, wispy pathways represent superficial and unconnected knowledge.

All knowledge and experience that an individual has is represented and connected in the brain. Some of these connections may be quite extensive (such as those involving knowledge and experience of life in a village, the roles and relationships of various members in the village, and village ceremonies); other connections may be very weak (such as knowledge about how a computer chip is

Drawing of the pathways through the brain. © John Allison/Peter Arnold, Inc.

made). The more extensive the connections, the more likely an individual is to understand something, to have it be meaningful, to remember it, and to access it for use in new situations. The weaker the connections, the less likely an individual will be able to recall or use the information.

Learning in depth provides increased opportunities for connections to be made. Another way to expand connections is to help students understand how new information connects to what they already know, to their lives, and to what they have previously learned in a particular subject and across subjects. Such connections are illustrated well in the grade 6 science text discussed earlier (McClenan & Morgan, 1989) in which 60 pages are devoted to the topic of light. In Figure 2, specific aspects of this text are highlighted to show how a book can be designed to encourage students to make connections.

In ways similar to those described in Figure 2, an effective teacher takes students' experiences and knowledge into account when designing learning activities. Through various approaches, students can be helped to see the links among what they already know, the new content, and the ways in which they can and should apply the new knowledge in other contexts.

FIGURE 2

How One Science Textbook Helps Students Make Connections

1. Each portion of a lesson begins with clearly stated objectives written in a language the students can understand, as in the following example:

   When you have completed this section, you should be able to

   - describe the kind of images formed by a lens that is thicker in the middle than at the edges;
   - compare the parts and functions of a camera to the eye; and
   - describe how our eyes work.

   Objectives can alert students to the parts of their prior knowledge and experience that will be activated during the upcoming lesson. It is similar to giving someone enough information so that he or she knows which drawer in a file cabinet to open.

2. Numerous activities relating to the topic being discussed in the text are offered. These activities provide additional opportunities for students to make connections, and because the activities involve students physically, students are able to increase the number of connections through their visual, tactile, and auditory senses. Each one of these ways of taking in and using information increases the number of connections related to a topic. Here is an example:

   What happens to straight rays of light when they pass through curved glass? Do this activity to find out....

3. Relevant illustrations, or drawings, throughout the text provide students with visual images to aid connections.

4. The text regularly connects the lesson to students' existing knowledge. For example, a unit on eyes and glasses begins with the following:

   Why do some people wear glasses? Is there anyone in your class or perhaps at home who wears eye glasses? Why do you think they wear them?... There are many things we can do to take care of the eyes, so that they will continue to work properly for a lifetime. While reading, watching television, or doing close work such as sewing, raise your eyes and look off into the distance occasionally to rest the eye muscles.

5. Students are explicitly shown the connections across lessons and topics, as in the following example:

   Earlier, you learned that the lenses form an image of things being looked at on the retina of each eye. Each image does not go away at once, but lasts for a short fraction of a second. The eye and the camera are like each other in the following ways....

(continued)

FIGURE 2 *(continued)*

6. Each of the main points in a lesson is summarized as the lesson proceeds, which allows students an additional opportunity to validate, refine, and correct connections.

   What have we learned? A convex lens is thicker in the middle than at the edges. A convex lens forms images by bending the light rays until they come together....

7. The text incorporates poetry throughout to illustrate various scientific principles. For example, a poem about trains by Robert Louis Stevenson is used to illustrate the concept of motion and energy, and a poem about rocks by a child helps students understand a chapter on rocks and soils. These poems can serve to enhance connections in several ways. First, the poem about trains helps students connect the abstract concepts of motion and energy with the concrete object and action of a train. Second, the poems help students make connections between the facts of science and their aesthetic sensibilities elicited by the poems. However, these sorts of connections must be obvious to the point of the text. If they are not, they will serve only to distract students.

8. The text engages students in creating or completing charts and graphs to help them classify the objects about which they are learning based on certain features. This helps students see how the various parts of a concept or principle are connected or how the various features of objects connect to form a classification system. Charts and graphs also show students how knowledge can be represented in different ways and may serve as visual images that may be easier to remember and to access later.

Science textbook excerpts from *First Steps in Science, Pupils' Book 6*, by V. McClenan and H. Morgan, 1989, Kingston, Jamaica: Longman.

Coherence in teaching. In 1985 a study was conducted to help explain the dramatic difference in scores on an international assessment of student achievement in mathematics (Travers et al., 1985). Classes containing students with consistently high scores were compared to classes containing students with consistently low scores. Although the researchers found a number of factors that could explain the differences in scores, they found coherence to be a major contributor to learning (Stigler & Perry, 1987).

Teachers of high-scoring students were much more likely to say and do things that would help students see the coherence of the mathematics lessons. For example, teachers explained how different segments of a lesson were related. They facilitated the transitions between segments of a lesson by encouraging discussions of how the segments were related, and they often initiated a lesson by explaining the goal of the day's class and how the activities were related to the goal. The teachers also explained how various activities were related to one another as a way of clarifying the principles that underlie different mathematical procedures. For example, one first-grade teacher asked a student, "Would you explain the difference between what we learned in the previous lesson and what you came across in preparing for today's lesson?" (Stigler & Perry, 1987, p. 217). The first-grade student was able to answer the question.

This study also found that teachers of high-scoring students tended to spend an entire 40-minute mathematics class period on the solution of only one, two, or three problems. Although the materials or activities throughout the lesson changed, the topics remained the same. It seems that the problems served as the link to tie the different instructional segments together.

Another major distinction between the high-scoring and low-scoring classes was the emphasis on thinking and reflection. The teachers of high-scoring students encouraged their students to think much more frequently and promoted reflection with questions such as, "Which is the best method? What do you notice here? Think about it with your partner. Think about the problem for a whole minute before beginning to solve it" (Stigler & Perry, 1987, p. 219). The teachers emphasized that the way a problem is worked is more important than the answer, and they urged their students to carry out procedures patiently, carefully, and precisely —not quickly.

In classrooms without coherence, instruction consisted mainly of a sequence of events that were strung together but had no explicit reference as to how the various events were related. Teachers often omitted any reference

to the topic or links to the students' experience. For example, in one classroom, the following lesson was observed:

OK, open your workbooks to page 12. I want you to measure your desk in pencils, find out how many pencils it takes to go across your desk, and write the answer on the line in your workbooks. [Children carry out instructions.] Next, see how many paper clips go across your desk, and write that number next to the paper clip in your workbook. [Children continue to follow instructions.] OK, the next line says to use green crayons, but we don't have green crayons so we are going to use blue crayons. Raise your hand if you don't have a blue crayon. [Teacher takes approximately 10 minutes to pass out blue crayons to students who raise their hands.] Now write the number of blue crayons next to the line that says green crayons. [Teacher then moves on to the third segment.] OK, now take out your centimeter ruler and measure the number of centimeters across your desk, and write the number on the line in your workbooks. (Stigler & Perry, 1987, p. 216–217)

The researchers note that the teacher does not indicate transition points, how each exercise helps students understand measurement, or why units are important. There is no reference to the goals of the class and how the activities relate to the goals. The researchers comment that the teacher took more time to hand out blue crayons than to convey the purpose of the three segments on measurement, and they argue that it would be difficult for the children to construct a coherent, meaningful account of this class.

Instead of connecting the activities required of the students to some central idea or theme, the teacher focused on the discrete units and failed to show the relations among the units.

The notion of coherence centers around the need for key ideas, or themes, and for showing how various parts connect to the whole. The themes serve as anchors to which students can connect the various bits and pieces of knowledge, skills, concepts, and ideas that are required for meaningful learning to occur. Themes allow for a richer set of connections in the student's mind than would less central ideas; the more connections and associations a learner has about a topic, the more understanding he or she has.

The importance of central ideas or themes in accessing and using knowledge suggests that instruction should be designed in a way that makes the central ideas explicit. It also suggests that to promote deep understanding and a rich connection of relations among information, the number of central ideas presented should be limited. The coherence and connection of the content should be clear to both students and teachers.

Organization. For knowledge to be coherent, it must be organized. However, the opposite is not true: knowledge can be organized but not be coherent. Organization has long been considered a key aspect of understanding, and in fact, the mathematician Polya (1973) considered the *organization* of one's knowledge to be even more important than the *extent* of it. Organization involves appropriately ordered relations among knowledge. According to those who study how memory works, knowledge is organized through links that connect various units of knowledge to form meaningful concepts and principles, much like telephone lines connect callers and allow them to communicate—if the telephone wires are not properly connected, people cannot speak with one another. Although it is possible for students to remember the units of knowledge they learn, they are not likely to access and use these bits and pieces of knowledge unless they are organized into a conceptual framework that connects all the pieces and gives the knowledge meaning.

Think of the memory as a file cabinet. If the files are carefully organized and labeled, it is much easier to find certain ones. But if papers are just placed randomly into the cabinet, a person must search through all the drawers and files to find information. This takes far too long and makes finding the right information difficult. Most people would simply give up and not bother. That is what students do when confronted with trying to learn information that is not organized in a way that is accessible.

The following paragraph from a science textbook has been rearranged. It may help illustrate the importance of organization for understanding:

> Some beetles help too. Earthworms eat decaying leaves, other plant parts, and soil. In what ways do you think they are useful? They pass out wastes into the soil. Remember both earthworms and ants make and live in holes in the soil. They bury dead animals and others move animal "droppings" or dung from place to place. Soil needs space for air and water to pass through.

A reader may be able to get the gist of this paragraph, but because the sentences have been rearranged, it is difficult to make sense of it. Here is the original organization:

> Animals such as worms and ants that live in the soil are very useful. In what ways do you think they are useful? Remember both earthworms and ants make and live in holes in the soil. Soil needs space for air and water to pass through. Earthworms eat decaying leaves, other plant parts, and soil. They pass out wastes into the soil. As they bore through the soil, earthworms also mix soil and break it into small pieces. Some beetles help too. They bury dead animals, and others move animal "droppings" or dung from place to place. (McClenan, Pottinger, & Gordon, 1990, p. 18)

The second paragraph is easier to comprehend. It is organized so that the main idea is stated in the first sentence to alert the reader to what follows. It asks a question to entice the reader to think about the ways that animals in soil might be useful, and then it supports the main idea with details.

Titles, headers, and tables of contents are mechanisms that facilitate comprehension of text. Graphs, tables, and charts are used to organize and display data. The way a teacher organizes and presents a lesson will influence how easily students can learn and access the information and connect the new information to what they already know.

Concepts and organization. One powerful way of organizing knowledge is through the use of concepts. Concepts are a collection of facts, principles, and ideas that are related to one another in specific ways and that have more explanatory power than do isolated facts. Concepts are the major structures for organizing knowledge and should be a primary focus in measuring students' understanding. A concept does not refer to a particular event or object (such as one particular planet) but represents features common to a category of events or objects; for example, "planet" is a concept in that all planets share the common features of being a body that shines by reflected sunlight and revolves around the sun. For students to understand the concept of a planet, they would need to understand the organization of how planets are related to the sun, how the light from the sun shines on the planets, and how the planets revolve around the sun.

If the concept of a planet were extended to the concept of a solar system, students would be required to not only know the names of the planets and the existence of a sun and a moon, but also understand the way that these objects of a solar system are organized and their relations to one another. Only when students understand these patterns and relations are they able to address more important scientific questions that derive from the understanding of a solar system, such as what planets are likely to be colder or hotter, which are likely to have life on them, what are the patterns of day and night, and how seasons of the year occur.

However, if an exam question simply asks students to list the nine planets in the solar system, students are not learning the more powerful, explanatory concept of a solar system. There is little they can do with simply knowing the names of the planets, yet this is often the type of question that they are asked. In fact, without even knowing the names of the planets, students could learn the patterns and relations of the solar system and begin to understand how these patterns and relations help explain the world. Conversely, students could memorize the names of the planets and have no real understanding of what a solar system is or how it affects their lives.

The following questions should be considered when designing a curriculum, writing a textbook, or developing a examination: Why should students know this? How is it important? What can they do with the knowledge? What kind of explanatory or problem-solving power does this knowledge or skill give them?

Improving testing and teaching through the use of conceptual models. One researcher (Mayer, 1989) has conducted numerous studies on conceptual models and has found them to be powerful learning tools. A brief description of these models and of the research findings in support of their use is included here because the implications for testing and teaching are direct and fairly easy to implement and could increase the amount of instruction that is focused on conceptual learning.

A conceptual model is words or diagrams intended to help learners build mental images of the system being studied and to make concepts and their relations more concrete. Systems that students might be learning about include radar, density, democratic systems, or social systems. A conceptual model highlights and organizes the main steps, elements, and states in the system (see Figure 3 for an example).

Mayer (1989) found that students who viewed a conceptual model for as little as one minute while reading a textual explanation of the material outperformed control students by a median of 57 percent in their ability to recall the concepts and by 64 percent in their ability to *use* the concepts to arrive at creative solutions to transfer problems. Mayer conducted 20 studies of conceptual models over 15 years and found consistently powerful results.

What may be even more intriguing is that the students who viewed the conceptual models actually scored a median of 14 percent lower on questions that measured verbatim retention, or recall. These findings suggest that students who perform better on recall tests may be less likely to use what they have learned to solve problems than students who do less well on recall tests. The results also may imply that those selected for higher levels of schooling based on tests that primarily measure recall may be less likely to use what they have learned to solve problems and that the students who are more likely to use their knowledge are not being selected. However, this could be determined only if the use of knowledge for solving problems is measured, which often is not the case.

Implications for testing. There are several ways that tests can be designed to promote coherence, connectedness, and organization. For example, if test questions ask students to organize and restructure what they have learned, students are more likely to learn in a way that helps them see how knowledge is organized and to file it in their "mental filing cabinets" in a way that they can remember and access later.

Restructuring knowledge helps students make more connections to what they already know and see a greater variety of ways the knowledge can be used. For example, to prepare for a science test, students could be asked

FIGURE 3

Conceptual Model Distinguishing Between Mass and Volume

Volume tells us how much space an object takes up. Finding the volume of an object is like finding how many individual cubes there are in a specific object. In the case below, volume is 3 x 4 x 2 = 24 cubes.

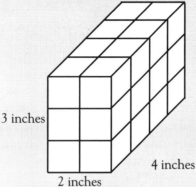

3 inches

4 inches

2 inches

We could theoretically even take one cube out.

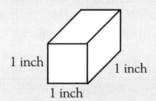

1 inch

1 inch

1 inch

Mass is the number of particles within an object. Some substances may have more particles in them than others. For example:

Box A
Mass = 3 particles

Box B
Mass = 6 particles

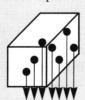

Box B has two times as many particles and thus twice the gravitational pull.

From "Models for Understanding," by R.E. Mayer, 1989, *Review of Educational Research, 59*, p. 52. Copyright 1989 by the American Educational Research Association. Reprinted by permission.

to scan the chapters in their textbook and identify the topics that involve energy. Answers might include animals and plants, food contributing to growth, light, heat, magnetism, sound, waves in the ocean, and rain. Or students could be asked to describe all the topics that involve cycles. Answers might include the cycles of night and day, months and years, sound, digestion, water cycle, and the influence of the moon on the ocean. In this way, even though the text might not directly address the broad but important themes of energy or cycles, if a teacher knows that questions such as these will be on the test, he or she is likely to work with students to analyze the text for such themes. Such questions would serve as an even more powerful learning experience if they asked students to explain why each of their selections was judged to be an example of energy or a cycle.

Tests should emphasize measuring concepts and principles more than factual knowledge. One way to do this is to have students draw a conceptual model, select a correct representation of a concept from among models, or fill in and label a partially completed conceptual model.

Questions that emphasize coherence also will encourage students to reflect rather than simply to recall. Reflection is defined in *Webster's Third New International Dictionary* as "consideration of some subject matter, idea, or purpose often with a view to understanding or accepting it or seeing it in its right relations or introspective contemplation of the contents or qualities of one's own thoughts or remembered experiences." Reflection not only helps students see the coherence of knowledge but also helps them understand things at

a deeper level. Students can be asked to connect the information being tested to their prior knowledge, lives, feelings, and thoughts or to other subjects or time periods. Examples provided in this chapter and throughout this book illustrate test questions that ask students to reflect and make connections.

Principle 3: Promote Active Learning

To expand the number of connections students make, teachers should give students a variety of ways to learn (such as talking, debating, acting, making models, and writing stories and reports). The more students' five senses are activated in learning, the more connections and representations that are related to new content can be made. Active learning stimulates more connections and is simply more fun. When learning is enjoyable, children want to come to school and are more likely to pay attention.

Learning in social settings, such as small groups, is motivating to students; it helps them articulate what they are learning and learn from one another. It also helps prepare students for the types of group tasks that they will encounter in their adult work lives. One study (Advancing Basic Education and Literacy, 1993) of an activity-based primary education kit being used in rural schools in India found the following:

> Attitudes of all involved have changed substantially. Children now enjoy school: they are more attentive and eager to learn. Teachers are much more enthusiastic. Even parents, who at first were quite concerned that their children were playing and not learning, noticed marked improvement in their children. Before the schools began using the activity kits, the classrooms were

filled with inertia and passive learning. The teacher droned. The child parroted. As a result, dropout rates were high, especially for girls. (p. 3)

Active learning takes more time than does reading the text, filling out worksheets, and answering recall questions. There is a tradeoff in the amount of information that can be addressed during a given time period and the amount of time allocated to active learning. The amount of material covered in the curriculum and textbooks is a critical factor teachers consider when determining if they can take time for active learning. If there is too much material to be covered, active learning will be discarded in favor of the quicker rote learning approach.

Implications for testing. Examinations can require students to be actively engaged in order to respond to questions. Many of the performance tasks discussed in later chapters require students to work individually, in pairs, or in small groups to solve problems. Hands-on science tasks are particularly useful ways to test students' science-process skills; these tasks communicate to teachers that they are expected to make activity-based, hands-on science a regular part of classroom instruction.

When children are allowed to be active learners, they are more likely to remember and use what they learn. Performance tests can help promote active learning. © Aga Khan Foundation/Jean-Luc Ray. Used by permission.

Principle 4: Use Real-Life Tasks

Often students do not automatically know how knowledge is used in situations that are different from the one in which the knowledge was learned. An important aspect of having an ability is its *transferability*. That is, students must be able to use what they learn in a variety of appropriate situations. For example, if students can subtract only when the mathematical function is presented as a number problem (such as 49–36=___), but cannot subtract when buying something at a market, then the skill is of little use. It is important that teachers, texts, and examinations all emphasize applying or transferring newly learned knowledge to various situations. Teachers should tell and show students explicitly how the new knowledge or concepts can be used in many situations, and they should give students practice in applying what they learn to real-life situations.

Transfer of knowledge can be promoted by having students produce written or illustrated comparisons that highlight common and important features across similar situations. For instance, students might be asked to compare situations in which it would be a good idea to estimate mathematically with those in which it would not.

Implications for testing. Several sample test questions provided later in this book relate to real-life experiences. One multiple-choice question asks students to indicate the weight of a fish lying in a scale. The question is designed to show students that if the scale is not initially set at "0," they are being cheated when they purchase goods in a market. Another test question engages students in comparing prices at a market to see which shop will save them the most money. Other questions ask students about health and environmental issues common in their region.

Principle 5: Make Students Aware of Their Learning

In a review of research to find out what factors are most likely to help students remember, access, and use knowledge, Prawat (1989) found that organization and awareness are two key elements. Students are more likely to access and use what they have learned if they are *aware* of what they know about a topic. Verbalizing or writing about content helps students reflect on their thoughts. Because much of our knowledge and many of our misconceptions and oversimplifications are tacit, speech and writing provide a means of becoming more aware of them. Writing and verbalizing help students see the inconsistencies in their thinking, which can help them resolve these inconsistencies. Any activity aimed at enhancing students' awareness should be consistent with the objectives of the lesson, and students should be reminded of these objectives—before, during, and after the lesson.

Students are more likely to understand something when they are required to explain, elaborate, or defend their positions to others because they must evaluate and integrate knowledge in new ways. Properly organized small-group learning can be effective in helping students become aware of their learning.

Implications for testing. To promote students' awareness of what they are learning, tests should ask students to write about the content in a way that helps them consolidate what they have learned; or they should direct students to compare common and dissimilar features across situations, such as patterns of trade in selected historical periods with current patterns of trade. Teachers can use assessment strategies in the classroom to help students identify gaps or inconsistencies in their understanding of a topic.

In Chapter 3 assessment portfolios are described. Sometimes students are asked to select pieces of their work for the portfolio; selections may be based on those pieces that represent the student's most significant growth in learning a subject. The process of reviewing and selecting their own work helps students become more aware of what they have learned. Students could be asked to explain in writing why they selected particular pieces. In all forms of assessment, students should be made aware of the criteria for good performance. In fact, it is useful to give students copies of the criteria that will be used to judge their performance. These criteria can help them be aware of their performance or understanding in relation to stated criteria for good performance.

Principle 6: Teach Students to Manage Their Learning

One of the descriptions of higher order thinking is that it involves a student in regulating his or her own thinking processes. Another description states that higher order thinking is not likely to occur when students are told what to do at every step; and a third description is that higher order thinking requires effort. Some students need to be taught how to manage their own learning. Teachers should give students opportunities to direct and manage their own learning and should make explicit what this involves. This is something that teachers may need to be taught how to do. Teachers also should encourage students to analyze their own and others' approaches to learning and discuss what they can do to be more efficient and effective learners. Students also should be encouraged to think about their learning over time.

Implications for testing. In one of the sample test items provided in a following chapter, students are asked to indicate what helps them understand what they read and how working in a group helps them understand and plan what they write. In another test item, students are told that they can underline and take notes in the test booklet to help them read the passage and write their responses to the questions. Both of these examples demonstrate appropriate ways to help students manage their learning.

A Summary

This chapter reviews some of the basic principles of good teaching and learning and discusses the implications of these principles for testing. The following factors are likely to foster students' abilities to access and apply knowledge in potentially relevant situations and should be promoted in teaching and learning through textbooks, teacher training, and testing:

- Make sure that instruction is coherent.
- Decrease the number of topics covered and provide more time to study important topics in depth.
- Use central ideas or themes to facilitate coherence in knowledge acquisition and use.

- Induce students to apply strategies for organizing and processing information.
- Encourage the learning of concepts.
- Provide opportunities that help students establish meaningful relations between new and prior knowledge.
- Encourage students to construct representations (through charts, graphs, drawings, tables, and conceptual models) that show the relations among the parts of a concept and of the parts to the whole concept.
- Provide more opportunities to use knowledge and skills in real-life situations.
- Provide time for students to verbalize and write about content.
- Give students opportunities to manage their own learning and to reflect on their learning.

Chapter 2 provides some definitions of technical terms and distinguishes between assessments and examinations, and between norm- and criterion-referenced tests. Chapter 3 shows how examination questions can be designed to be consistent with the principles of better teaching and learning described in this chapter.

CHAPTER 2

Examinations, Assessments, and Continuous Assessment: Differences and Uses

This chapter clarifies relevant testing terminology and explains several concepts that are critical to understanding the appropriate use of tests. Specifically, the terms assessment, measurement, and test are defined; and specific instances of each are described, including national assessment and continuous assessment and norm- and criterion-referenced tests. In addition, the terms validity and reliability are explained.

Assessment

Assessment is a broad category that encompasses both measurement and tests. Assessment is defined as a *process* for obtaining information that is used for making decisions about students, curricula, programs, and educational policy (Nitko, 1996). The decisions made with assessment information may concern the following (see also Figure 4):

- students, such as whether a student needs additional instruction in a topic;

- programs, such as whether a trial math program is effective in developing students' problem-solving abilities; or

- educational policy, such as whether a policy that requires students to be pro-

moted to the next grade is more or less detrimental than a policy that allows low-achieving students to be retained.

This chapter will address two major types of assessment—national assessment and continuous assessment. A national assessment is designed and used to compare the performance of educational *systems* such as schools, districts, states, provinces, or nations. Results generally are not collected or reported at the individual student level but rather on the school or classroom level within a region.

Continuous assessment is an essential part of the teaching and learning process and operates at the classroom level. It is a systematic way that teachers can determine how well their students have learned what has been taught. It may consist of various measures that a teacher can use to tell whether his or her instruction has been effective and to pinpoint students who have or have not mastered particular skills. In some cases, the information collected through continuous assessment is used with external test scores to make certification or selection decisions. Both national and continuous assessment are described in detail later in this chapter.

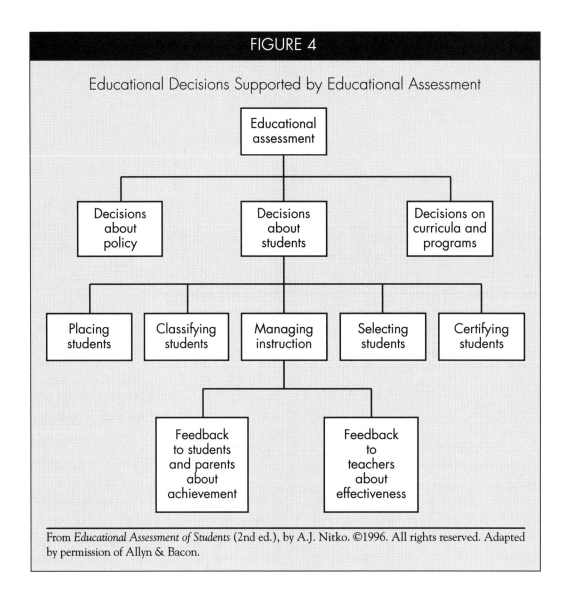

FIGURE 4

Educational Decisions Supported by Educational Assessment

From *Educational Assessment of Students* (2nd ed.), by A.J. Nitko. ©1996. All rights reserved. Adapted by permission of Allyn & Bacon.

Measurement

Gathering information for the assessment process usually involves measurement. Measurement is defined as a *procedure* for assigning numbers to a specified attribute (Nitko, 1996). Measurement tools are quite varied and can include using a ruler to measure a piece of wood, a dipstick to measure the amount of oil in a car, or a test to measure how much learning has occurred. An important characteristic of measurement is that the marks obtained through measuring should maintain the relations that exist in the real world. So, for example, a dipstick that accurately measures the amount of oil in the car is necessary; we want to know if and when we need to add oil, and if so, how much we need to add. In measuring student learning, the measures should be able to distinguish accurately among students who, for example, know how to read well, can barely read, or are unable to read.

Blalock (1968) describes four steps in the measurement process:

1. Define what is to be measured.

2. Select or develop the measurement tool that is consistent with the definition of what is to be measured.

3. Obtain empirical information for the indicators.

4. Evaluate the validity of the indicators —to what degree the indicators represent the concept, skill, or behavior to be measured.

Test

A test is a specific instrument or systematic procedure for observing and describing one or more characteristics using either a numerical scale or a classification scheme. Tests can involve either paper and pencil instruments or observations. Or, for example, students' ability to do a research project can be tested by having them do a project and classifying their projects according to preestablished criteria. Tests can be used in the classroom to make decisions about individual students, within the context of a national assessment to make judgments and decisions about student learn-ing at the school or district level, or by national or regional bodies to make decisions about individual students for certification, selection, or promotion. In this book, the term *examination* will be used to refer to tests used at the end of a cycle (a specified period of learning, such as primary school) to make determinations regarding certification, selection, or promotion, as mentioned in the introduction.

Norm-Referenced and Criterion-Referenced Testing

Tests can be either norm referenced or criterion referenced. Traditional testing conceptions and technology were developed for use with norm-referenced tests to help make comparison and selection decisions. However, during the 1960s and 1970s, educators noticed that there were certain shortcomings with using norm-referenced tests for making instructional decisions. Criterion-referenced testing technology was developed to counteract some of the shortcomings of norm-referenced testing technology.

The purpose of norm-referenced tests is to compare student performance on a test with that of a norm group of students, but not to determine how proficient a student is in a particular subject, skill, or concept. (Norm-referenced tests are also used to make comparisons among school systems. In this instance, scores are reported for schools, districts, regions, or nations but not for individual students. The same shortcomings that apply to norm-referenced test use for individual students also apply for systems or subsystems.) Criterion-referenced tests are designed to determine whether an individual has learned specific skills or knowledge.

There are two main differences in the way that norm- and criterion-referenced tests are designed and used. Norm-referenced tests are often used to make selection decisions and are designed to spread examinees out along a continuum, so that those who score at the highest end of the continuum can be selected. That is, the students who score high on the test are placed at one end of the continuum, those who score low are placed at the other end, and those who score in between are placed in the middle of the continuum. In order to spread the examinees out, test makers need items, or questions, that distinguish between high- and low-scoring students. That is, students who score high on the overall test should get the item correct, and students who score low on the overall test should get the item wrong.

This approach to test design may work against good teaching and learning. If teachers are teaching a topic well and students are learning it well, most students will answer a test item on that topic correctly. However, if most students answer an item correctly, then the item no longer serves to discriminate between high- and low-scoring students, and the test makers will need to discard that item from the test. Therefore, whatever gets taught and learned well is ultimately removed from the test. Although this serves the process of selection well, it undermines effective teaching and learning and is more likely to reward native intellectual ability rather than hard work. This practice also risks making the test less representative of the overall curriculum and of some of the intended outcomes of education.

A second major distinction between norm- and criterion-referenced tests is the amount of description that is provided about what the test is measuring and how it is being measured by the test. The amount of description provided for a norm-referenced test is generally quite sparse. This makes it difficult for teachers and policymakers to be clear about what students know or can do, which undermines the usefulness of the test results for improvement efforts.

A critical feature of a well-designed criterion-referenced test is the use of more detailed descriptions in the form of item, or domain, specifications. Item specifications are descriptions of the skills, concepts, or knowledge being measured, including allowable content, level of difficulty, and test-item format. They are written typically for each of the subskills being measured on the test. If properly prepared, specifications also can enhance the validity and reliability of a test. Criterion-referenced tests and specifications are described in more detail in Chapter 7.

In summary, norm-referenced tests can be useful for selection or comparison purposes, but they also can have an adverse effect on instruction. Criterion-referenced tests can be used for selection or comparison purposes if norms are established and there is sufficient variation in students' performance.

Selection Examinations

Selection examinations are used to make decisions about which of many applicants are best suited for a particular opportunity—usually a higher level of schooling. In developing countries, the selection process often begins at the end of primary school. Selection examinations can be measures of either achievement or aptitude; each has advantages and disadvantages and both are likely to influence teaching and learning.

Achievement tests. Achievement tests measure what students have learned in school. Sometimes they are given locally, such as within regions or states or by the school or university to which the student is applying. In other situations, they are given by a central body, such as a ministry of education or an examining board. When all students take the same test set by a central body, it is possible to compare the performances across test takers. When students in different parts of a country take different tests, or when students take a centrally developed test but are allowed to answer different questions, comparability is not possible. Comparability is an important issue that will be discussed more fully later.

Aptitude tests. There are several meanings for the word "aptitude": one is an individual's aptitude, or inclination, for a particular career; another refers to aptitude for learning or aptitude for success at higher levels of schooling. Different measures are used for career aptitude than are used for learning aptitude. Aptitude tests used to assess learning potential measure general academic principles that would be found in a typical curriculum, but they are *not* designed to measure the content of any specific curriculum. They are similar to tests of general intelligence; the types of questions included on an aptitude test might involve abstract reasoning and symbol manipulation, skills considered necessary for success at higher levels of learning.

The Scholastic Assessment Test (SAT), previously called the Scholastic Aptitude Test, developed in the United States is a well-known example. It is used widely for university selection in the United States, primarily because each of the nation's 16,000 school districts has its own curriculum, which precludes use of an achievement test written to measure a specific curriculum. Although some states in Australia use the SAT, most of the selection examinations used in Europe and Africa are achievement tests.

Aptitude tests have been criticized because they are a less accurate predictor of academic success at the college or university level than are achievement measures and because they tend to reward native intellectual ability rather than diligence and hard work. Some consider this latter feature to be a benefit because it is believed that the aptitude test is able to identify bright, disadvantaged students who may come from impoverished schools and homes. Not everyone agrees with this assertion, and there are many who believe that aptitude tests are detrimental to students from some minority groups. In addition, a test that purports to measure native intellectual ability can penalize students who may have a lower intellect but work harder to achieve.

The most serious concern about examinations used for selection purposes—both achievement and aptitude—is the powerful influence that they have on teaching and learning. Because the consequences of performing well on a selection examination are so critical to students, teachers, and parents, a tremendous amount of time, attention, and effort is devoted to preparing for the exam. If the examination does not reflect the curriculum, it is likely that the exam will replace the curriculum. If the examination does not measure what policymakers and others believe is important for students to know, it is likely that it will be neglected in the classroom.

Another problem with selection examinations is that because there is generally very little description of what is being measured, teachers and students resort to memorizing questions from previous tests. Enterprising entrepreneurs in many countries produce and sell exam-preparation books that comprise collections of items from previous exams. This may serve as a disincentive for students to learn the underlying concepts and principles, which are far more generalizable and powerful units of knowledge; instead, students tend to acquire unrelated fragments of knowledge without understanding how they are connected into a coherent and useful knowledge structure.

Improving examinations. There are several steps that can be taken to counter the negative influences of selection examinations on teaching and learning and to design and use these examinations in a way that is more likely to have a positive effect. These steps, described more fully later, are as follows:

1. Use a criterion-referenced approach to developing examinations.

2. Disseminate information about what will be tested and how it will be tested.

3. Report test results in a way that guides instructional improvement.

4. Test fewer, more important skills and knowledge that measure students' abilities to integrate and apply what they have learned.

5. Build quality-control mechanisms into the test development and scoring procedures.

Subsequent chapters contain descriptions of what quality examinations should look like, who should be involved in the development of examinations, and how and what to communicate about the exams in order to promote improved teaching and learning.

National Assessment and Continuous Assessment

National assessment is a process in which various measures are used to gather data for the purpose of monitoring school systems. National assessment generally is designed to collect data on a number of variables of interest, including the number of students enrolled, student-teacher ratios, retentions, and drop-outs. These types of variables are referred to as input variables—the factors that go into the system. Output variables are the consequences, or outcomes, of the system, such as student achievement. Although most school systems collect many types of input data, relatively few nations collect measures of the outputs of their school systems.[1]

In a report to the Board on International Comparative Studies in Education, Puryear (1993) noted,

The statistics that countries regularly gather, even when reliable, fail to cover some of the most fundamental aspects of education. Most resources have been dedicated to a single approach to monitoring educational systems: counting the inputs. Governments have concentrated almost entirely on recording the number of teachers, pupils, and buildings in the formal system, and the size of public educational expenditures. They have given virtually no attention to documenting how schools function or what students learn. Therefore much of the data that could help determine where scarce educational resources ought to be allocated, or how effectively they are being used, are simply not on hand. (p. 5)

In addition, the process of the educational system—what goes on in classrooms—is seldom measured. Although measuring is a costly and time-consuming aspect of assessment, it is essential to accurately understanding some of the more subtle constraints on teaching and learning, which would not be evident even with achievement data. However, student achievement data can help target schools and subjects that should be studied through classroom observations and can aid in more cost-effective data collection of process variables. In addition, this input and process, or contextual, data may help explain why schools obtain the outcomes they do. Chapter 8 provides more detail on collecting information regarding some of the process and contextual variables that help explain student achievement results.

When an assessment system does include measures of student achievement, results are reported typically at the system and subsystem levels instead of at the individual student level. This means that a test can be administered to a sample of schools or classrooms within a region rather than to every student. The fact that assessments can be administered on a sample basis allows greater flexibility in the types of measures that can be used. For example, performance tasks that require hand scoring are more feasible when only a sample of students are assessed. In addition to reporting on student performance in schools, districts, or regions, assessment results also may be used to report differences between rural and urban areas, boys and girls, and other student achievement factors.

How National Assessments and Examinations Differ

National assessments, in the form of achievement tests, differ from end-of-cycle examinations in several ways (see Table 1). Because they are concerned with assessing the performance of the system or subsystem, assessments generally are administered to a sample of students (as few as 2,000 to 3,000 students per grade) rather than to every student, as mentioned. Assessment scores are analyzed, interpreted, and reported by groups (for example, by classroom, schools, districts, and/or gender) instead of by individual students. And, assessments often are conducted every two or three years rather than every year and administered only in the core subject areas of language arts (reading and writing), mathematics, and science. In addition, assessments are seldom administered at every grade or class but instead once or twice at the primary level, once in the middle grades, and again at the secondary level. For example, an assessment of mathematics may be administered to one grade per level (in grades 4, 8, and 11) in one year; an assessment of reading and writing administered to these same grades the following year; and an assessment of science learning in the third year. The cycle would then begin again the following year with another mathematics as-

TABLE 1

Differences Between National Assessments and Examinations

	National Assessments	Examinations
Administered to	a sample of students	individual students
Level of report	school, district, region, or nation	individual students
Frequency	every 2 or 3 years per subject	every year
Subjects tested	math, science, reading, and writing	all in curriculum
Administered at	usually one grade per cycle (for example, grades 4, 8, and 11)	end of schooling cycle

sessment. The benefit of this approach is that it provides a measure of trends over time and does not overburden either the schools or the administering agency.

However, documenting trends over time is only possible if the measures remain consistent. This does *not* mean that the same items must be used each time the test is administered; it means that the same skills should be measured in the same way and at the same level of difficulty each time. This provides comparability from one administration to the next and allows policymakers to gauge the effects of their efforts to make improvements in the system. The use of item specifications, described in Chapter 7, provides a way to develop collections, or banks, of test items that can be used from year to year and that measure the same skill or content each time the tests are given. (Statistical techniques can also be used to equate items on various forms of a multiple-choice test.)

National assessment tests can be designed using either a norm-referenced or criterion-referenced approach. However, the most suitable approach for influencing better teaching and learning is to develop criterion-referenced tests and to provide normative data. This allows for descriptions of what students can and cannot do and for comparisons across classrooms, schools, and districts.

Continuous Assessment

Continuous assessment is a student evaluation system that operates at the classroom level and is integrated with the instructional process. It may consist of a variety of measures and procedures that a teacher can use to tell whether his or her instruction has been effective and to target those students who have and have not mastered particular skills. It serves as the foundation for improved instruction in the classroom.

Continuous assessment can be formal or informal. Teachers informally assess their students daily, either by observing them, asking questions, or giving tests and quizzes. Formal continuous assessment systems are sometimes used when a common set of classroom measures are developed centrally for use by an entire school system. The measures are administered and used by teachers at the classroom level, but the assessment system is formalized by standardizing the instruments and procedures across teachers and classrooms and sometimes includes centralized or regional monitoring.

The interest in continuous assessment has increased in developing countries. Many countries have begun to use course grades in conjunction with end-of-cycle examination marks to make promotion, certification, and selection decisions. The advantage of doing this is to increase the emphasis on the day-to-day learning that occurs in the classroom and to increase the accuracy of the selection and certification decisions. Examination marks alone provide an incomplete picture of what a student has learned and emphasize only one aspect of a complex set of understandings, knowledge, and skills. The greater the number of assessments that are used in making judgments about students, the greater the likelihood that the judgments will be accurate.

How is a continuous assessment system initiated? There are several ways to institute a continuous assessment system. Some countries simply exhort teachers to assess their students on a regular basis and may provide them with a sheet or card for recording students' marks. However, there are limitations to providing only the cards for recording students' marks without a common set of measures. There is little consistency in the marks assigned by teachers or in the assessments used to assign the marks. In addition, many teachers have not been trained well in classroom assessment, so they may not be doing an adequate job of using assessment in the classroom. In fact, some teachers may not be assessing at all. Most teachers in developing countries are underpaid, undertrained, and overworked. Many have two shifts of classes, often with too many students per class, so they may be disinclined to spend additional time outside of class developing tests, quizzes, or other approaches to assessing their students. Another concern is that when course grades begin to count toward selection decisions, teachers are vulnerable to corruption.

For these reasons, some countries are considering a continuous assessment system that would be developed at the central level and would provide all teachers with a common set of assessments. This would involve developing a series of assessments for topics, skills, and lessons within the curriculum for each grade or class. Classroom-based assessments are far more amenable to the authentic types of assessments discussed later in this book—projects, portfolios, performance tasks, and small-group work—so if they are well conceived, they can be a powerful way to influence the quality of teaching and learning in the classroom.

For example, assume that the lesson objective is to "apply principles of prevention and care for common accidents and unsafe situations in the local environment." There are many ways to assess students in relation

If continuous classroom-based assessments are well conceived, they can be a powerful way to influence the quality of teaching and learning. © Aga Khan Foundation/Jean-Luc Ray. Used by permission.

to this objective. Students can be asked to observe activity in their homes and identify and record unsafe situations that may lead to accidents. They can bring in their observations and share them with their peers in small groups. After sharing, the students in the small group can combine their observations and present an integrated list. At this point there are three possible sources for assessment: individual student records, group records, and ratings of students' interaction in groups. (Figure 5 is a guide for scoring students' group participation.) Students can then repeat the activity in their neighborhoods and communities and be asked to work in their groups to develop informational and advocacy campaigns and materials to promote the prevention of accidents and unsafe situations. They can create posters and arrange to make presentations at community council meetings.

In an activity such as this, students can learn many skills and concepts, including those listed on page 36.

FIGURE 5

Guide for Scoring Students' Group Participation

Student name _____

	Almost always	Often	Sometimes	Rarely
1. Group participation				
Participated in group without prompting.				
Did his or her fair share of the work.				
Tried to dominate the group—interrupted others or spoke too much.				
Participated in the group's activities.				
2. Staying on the topic				
Paid attention, listened to what was being said and done.				
Made comments aimed at getting the group back to the topic.				
Got off the topic or changed the subject.				
Stayed on the topic.				
3. Offering useful ideas				
Gave ideas and suggestions that helped the group.				
Offered helpful criticism and comments.				
Influenced the group's decisions and plans.				
Offered useful ideas.				
4. Consideration				
Made positive, encouraging remarks about group members and their ideas.				
Gave recognition and credit to others for their ideas.				
Made inconsiderate or hostile comments about a group member.				
Was considerate of others.				

(continued)

FIGURE 5 (continued)

	Almost always	Often	Sometimes	Rarely
5. Involving others				
Got others involved by asking questions, requesting input, or challenging them.				
Tried to get the group working together to reach group agreements.				
Seriously considered the ideas of others.				
Involved others.				
6. Communicating				
Spoke clearly—was easy to hear and understand.				
Communicated clearly.				

Giving students this form ahead of time and discussing it with them will ensure that they understand what is expected of them when they work with others in small groups. It is much more likely that they will engage in appropriate, supportive group behavior.

From *Assessment as an Opportunity to Learn: The Connecticut Common Core of Learning Alternative Assessment of Secondary School Science and Mathematics*, by J.B. Baron (Ed.), 1993, Hartford, CT: Connecticut State Department of Education. Reprinted by permission.

■ sources of accidents and accident prevention;

■ skills of observation, recording, synthesizing, and reporting data;

■ group skills such as sharing the work, not dominating the group, paying attention, staying on the topic, being considerate of others and others' ideas, and communicating clearly;

■ how to communicate with and persuade various audiences;

■ how to solve problems; and

■ how to take responsibility for making their community a better place to live.

However, teachers who are not well trained may have difficulty in determining the criteria for judging students on the objectives outlined, which is one of the benefits of a centrally developed continuous assessment system. Individuals who receive appropriate training and have time to develop the assessments would be able to develop more creative, pedagogically and technically sound assessments. They could develop as-

sessments that support independent and re-
sourceful learning, higher order thinking,
and problem solving; that are consistent with
the principles of learner-centered instruction; that have objective criteria for evaluating student performance; that involve children in applying the knowledge, skills, and
concepts to solving real-life problems in their
communities; and that lead to instruction
that captivates children's interest and imagination. This level of sophistication is unlikely for most classroom teachers, and the assessments they create themselves may tend
to reinforce rote learning.

The Namibia Ministry of Education and
Culture (1995) has produced a helpful description of continuous assessment for the
teacher's guide to the syllabus for grade 5 natural science and health education. A copy of
this section of the guide is in Appendix A.
In addition, Namibia's continuous assessment
guide for teachers of social studies contains
several scales that help teachers assign marks
for various types of competencies (Namibia
Ministry of Education and Culture, 1994).
One of the scales is particularly notable because it assigns the higher marks to the application of knowledge and understanding to
new situations. By articulating this in the
marking scheme, it draws teachers' attention
to the importance of helping students apply
what they have learned.

*Who should develop a continuous assess-
ment system?* Because continuous assessment
systems should reflect the curriculum and
textbooks, curriculum staff trained in assessment may be the most qualified and appropriate for developing continuous assessments
and for conducting training associated with

the continuous assessment system. Although
it is costly to involve all teachers in the development process, there are several benefits
that indicate there should be as much teacher
involvement as possible, as follows.

- The assessment skills teachers learn will
  help them to be more effective in assessing and remediating their students
  on a day-to-day basis.

- The process of writing specifications,
  assessment tasks, or test items engages
  teachers in discussions with their colleagues about what they are teaching,
  how they are teaching it, and how students are learning the content. This is
  one of the few opportunities teachers
  have to discuss with one another the
  content and process of teaching and
  learning.

- Teachers are more likely to support the
  continuous assessment system if they
  are part of the development process.
  Anecdotal reports from Swaziland indicate that teachers who were involved
  believed that it was quite useful to improve their test-development skills.

Validity and Reliability

Over the past century, there have been
three major trends in the design and use of
tests. During the early part of this century,
several innovations were developed to increase the technical sophistication of norm-
referenced tests. In fact, the technical foundation of testing was developed during this time
and serves as the basis for most graduate-level
training programs in measurement. However,
in the 1960s and 1970s educators and psycho-

metricians began to see that the use of norm-referenced tests was having a detrimental effect on teaching and learning. Criterion-referenced testing technology was developed to counteract these negative influences and to create a testing technology that was more compatible with the teaching and learning process. Over the past 25 years, the emergence of cognitive and brain research has led to yet a third shift in the views and uses of tests: this trend focuses on designing tests that are more compatible with what research says about how individuals learn, think, and solve problems. This type of testing is often referred to as authentic assessment.

There are certain technical criteria that are essential to all three generations of tests—most notably, the concepts of validity and reliability. Although all tests should be valid and reliable, the specific types of validity or reliability that are appropriate for any given test use may vary. Many of the technical approaches used for the more traditional, norm-referenced tests are inappropriate for the new forms of authentic assessment highlighted in this book, such as performance tasks, open-ended questions, and portfolios. The concepts of validity and reliability are undergoing reconceptualization for the current generation of authentic assessments. This task is complicated by the fact that some tests are designed to serve more than one purpose, such as both selection and instructional improvement. Validity and reliability are two technical issues that are changing as the nature of the testing process changes.

Although validity and reliability may seem peripheral to the concerns of educa-tional policymakers, they are really quite essential. If a test is used in an invalid way, or if it does not produce reliable estimates of the test taker's abilities, then the use of the test, particularly if it is used for making selection decisions, may be undermining other efforts to improve the educational system and to promote economic and social development. For example, if a selection examination is not accurately predicting which students will perform better at the next level of education, then it may be denying the most able students the opportunity to prepare for positions of leadership. If a test does not elicit reliable, or consistent, results, then an able student may be selected on one occasion and a mediocre student the next. The less reliable a test is, the more capricious the decisions that will be made based on the results.

If educational policymakers understand the principles of validity and reliability, they will be able to ensure that the people more directly responsible for testing are preparing and using tests in ways that are valid, reliable, and fair. The following section provides brief descriptions of the various types of validity and reliability.

Validity

Validity is the extent to which a test measures what it purports to measure; it is concerned primarily with the *interpretations* of data that arise from using the test rather than with the test itself. A test itself is not valid or invalid; rather, it is the inferences and decisions that are made based on the test results that are valid or invalid. Determining validity involves asking and answering questions such as the following.

- Do the scores actually reflect what they set out to measure?
- Are accurate decisions being made on the basis of the test scores?
- Is a student who receives a certificate proficient in the skills and knowledge that most would expect from that level of education?
- Is a student who is selected to attend secondary school more able than another student who is not selected?

Use of the test results is the key to understanding validity. A test may be developed in a technically sound way, but if it is used inappropriately, then it is not valid. For example, using a test of mechanical abilities to select individuals for jobs as school administrators would not be a valid use of the test, even though it may be a perfectly sound test of mechanical abilities.

There are several types of validity, and determining which types are needed will vary with the type of test and the intended uses of the test. Some of the types of validity include content validity, curricular and instructional validity, and predictive validity. A test may have or need only one type of validity.

Content validity. Content validity means that the items or tasks on a test represent the subject-matter content the test is intended to sample. This includes questions such as, "Does the test measure all relevant aspects of the subject domain?" The subject domain could be as small as multiplication of single-digit numbers or as expansive as primary-level mathematics.

Content validity is related partly to curricular issues. However, many of the subject-matter curricula are being reconceptualized. For example, in the area of reading, comprehension was traditionally conceived as understanding the main idea and the details of a text. However, recent research-based conceptualizations of reading comprehension have added other, more subtle, yet important types of comprehension such as "inferential comprehension" and "interpretative comprehension." If a test of reading does not include these other dimensions of comprehension, it may not be considered to have content validity. Content validity is difficult to establish but should involve various groups such as subject-matter experts, curriculum specialists, and educational researchers in the subject area in decisions regarding the content validity of a test (American Psychological Association, 1985). In order to make these decisions, these experts should be knowledgeable about recent research-based changes in the views of how various subjects are taught and learned.

Curricular and instructional validity. Two other types of validity are curricular and instructional validity. Curricular validity means that the test measures what is contained in the curriculum; instructional validity means that students are receiving instruction in the skills and knowledge being measured on the test and in the way they are measured on the test.

It is clear that content, curricular, and instructional validity are interrelated. However, this does not mean that if one type of validity is established, the others will follow. For example, some skill or concept may be in the curriculum, but it may not be taught or not taught as intended. This may be because teachers do not know how to teach it, or perhaps they do not have time to teach it because there is too much to cover in the curriculum. In this instance, the test would have curricular validity but not instructional validity.

Predictive validity. When using a test for selection purposes, the intent is to predict which students will be successful at the next level of education. In order to predict accurately, it is necessary to conduct studies to determine the relation, or correlation, between the measure used to predict (the selection test or school grades) and success in what is being predicted, such as secondary or university school performance. Without such evidence, it is impossible to know if the students who are most likely to be successful at the next level of schooling are being selected. This is exemplified in a report by Kellaghan and Greaney (1992) who note the following concerning the 14 African countries studied by the World Bank:

> Despite the emphasis on selection in public examinations, study of the predictive validity of performance on the examinations has received little attention. The limited available evidence is not very encouraging. In one study in Ethiopia, students' performance on the ESLCE [Ethiopian School Leaving Certificate Examination] mathematics examination did not predict success in first-year mathematics in the university (Asmerson and others, 1989). A somewhat similar study conducted by the University of Zambia concluded that the low predictive validity of examinations rendered their use for selection at all levels problematic (Kelly, 1986). (p. 46)

In the developed world, numerous studies have been conducted to estimate the predictive validity of various selection tests.

Choppin (1990) reports that when scholastic assessment tests developed in North America are used outside North America, they are less accurate in their predictions, and the effectiveness of the predictions varies by subject areas.

Changes in Conceptions of Validity

Recently, criteria for determining the validity of a test have been elaborated to be consistent with the new uses of tests as tools for influencing teaching and learning (Baker, O'Neil, & Linn, 1993). Tests that are intended to influence better teaching and learning should exhibit the following characteristics. They should

- have meaning for students and teachers and motivate high performance;
- require that students demonstrate complex thinking processes, such as problem solving, knowledge representation, and explanation, and be applicable to important problem areas;
- exemplify current standards of content or subject-matter quality;
- minimize the effects of ancillary skills that are irrelevant to the focus of the assessment; and
- state explicit standards for scoring students' performance. (p. 1214)

When the results of the tests are available, additional questions should be answered:

- Is the assessment sensitive to instruction—does it measure competencies that can be taught and learned?

- Is the assessment fair to students of different backgrounds?

- Is there evidence of a relation to other relevant performance; for example, do students perform similarly in course grades or on other measures of related skills or knowledge?

- Are the cost and administrative requirements of administering and scoring the test feasible?

- What are the consequences of the test on various aspects of the educational system? Are there unanticipated and unintended outcomes of the assessment? (Baker, O'Neil, & Linn, 1993, p. 1214)

To answer many of these questions will require classroom-based studies. These studies are essential to the testing process but are often neglected. Educational researchers from universities may be helpful to assist in conducting such studies. Involving teachers as researchers in their own classrooms and schools is another useful strategy, which also will engage teachers in the process of reflecting on the teaching and learning process.

Reliability

Reliability refers to consistency—does the test yield the same results on repeated administrations, or do different judges marking a test arrive at the same mark? A test is considered reliable if

- the student performs about the same when reexamined with the same test at a different time (without additional instruction);

- the student obtains the same score on a different form of the same test; or

- consistent decisions are made using the test results.

Obtaining reliability means eliminating imperfections in the test or testing situation that preclude accurate estimates of student behavior. There are several factors that can influence how a student performs on a test, factors that are not related to what or how much the student knows but that can influence the student's score. These factors include the following:

- the testing situation—for example, is it very noisy in the testing hall?

- the test administrator—for instance, does the administrator give hints about the test or unclear directions?

- variations in different forms of the same test—are items on one form slightly easier than on the other?

- instructions for taking the test—are they clear, and is the test format familiar to students?

As with validity, there are several types of reliability, and these types may vary depending on the type of test used. In most cases, several or all of these forms of reliability should be checked and adjustments made as needed.

Test-retest reliability. If the same student took the test at two different times, would he or she receive approximately the same score (assuming there was no additional learning between test administrations)? For example, if the test gave students a choice of answering several optional essay questions, their scores may vary depending on which question they selected.

Alternate-forms reliability. If a different but similar test was used, would students receive the same score? A number of studies have shown that different forms of the same test can result in different scores for the same student, even though both forms of the test intend to measure the same content.

Intermarker (or interrater) reliability. If three people read an essay or mark (score) a performance task, will they assign the same mark? Some procedures used to mark essays are not likely to result in consistent ratings of students' work. For example, if examinations are given to individual teachers to mark without benefit of either criteria for marking, training in marking, or checks for consistency with other markers, it is likely that the marks assigned will be inconsistent and therefore unreliable.

Sufficient-item reliability. With multiple-choice questions, reliability involves having a sufficient number of questions measuring the skill to get a reliable estimate of a student's performance on that skill. (This is also a concern with essays, short-answer questions, and performance tasks.) On a multiple-choice question with four response options ("a" through "d"), the student has a 25 percent chance of guessing the correct answer. With only three response options, the chance of guessing correctly increases to 33 percent. If there are only two questions measuring a skill, such as subtraction, then it is difficult to confirm that the student has actually mastered the skill even if the student gets both questions correct. In general, the longer the test, the more reliable the results.

The Need to Ensure Validity and Reliability

In a review of examinations systems in 14 African countries, the World Bank (Kellaghan & Greaney, 1992) cited a number of serious problems with the examinations. Most of them showed serious weaknesses in either content or instructional validity, and the issue of test reliability had not been adequately addressed. Important decisions are made based on these examinations, and all concerned are entitled to be confident that the measures that are being used to make these decisions are technically sound.

How to Ensure the Validity of Certifications

Increase the number of items tested per skill. When an education agency certifies a student, it means that the student has learned a specific set of skills, concepts, and knowledge specified in the curriculum. The validity of these certifications is important to many individuals—schools accepting incoming students, employers, parents, and the students themselves. It is important that these various groups have confidence that students being certified are proficient in the skills and knowledge deemed important for them to know (for example, reading, writing, and computing). This means that each subject-matter test should consist of a separate subtest for each of the *significant* skills, concepts, or knowledge of concern and that students should demonstrate that they are proficient in each of these essential skill areas. Five to twelve items per skill area allow decision makers to be more confident about a student's proficiency in the skills being certified. Fewer items are needed if the skill is being measured using a performance task or written composition because there is little chance that a student could get the correct answer by guessing. However, recent research on the generalizability of performance tasks estimates that five or six tasks are needed to be able to generalize proficiency in the broader skill rather than to only the tasks used on the test. For example, using a performance task that measures students' understanding of electrical circuits cannot generalize to their understanding of all the content covered in the grade 6 science curriculum.

Raise the passing scores. Passing scores also are important in providing valid certifications of students' proficiency. Passing scores are as low as 30 percent in some countries. A score this low does *not* indicate that the student has mastered the skills, knowledge, or concepts tested. If passing scores are too low, the educational system is allowing students to graduate without having mastered essential skills. *It is better to ensure that all students have learned a few highly important skills or concepts well than many superficially or not at all.* Passing scores should be high for each of the subtests that measure essential skills or knowledge—high enough that independent judges would consider the student to be proficient in the skill. In skills or topics that are less essential, somewhat lower scores may be acceptable.

Often a passing score is set for a whole test, such as a math test. Such tests often contain only one or two items per skill area, such as addition, story problems, or measurement. This means that the test can measure 50 to 100 different skills, concepts, or facts. If the passing score of 60 percent is set on the overall test, it would mean that a student who received a score of 60 percent *did not know* 40 percent of the skills in the specific curriculum measured by the test. Moreover, if the test is multiple choice, it is possible that the student may not know another 25 to 30 percent of the items he or she answered correctly because there is a 25 to 30 percent chance of correctly guessing on these types of items. This means that a student may be certified who may have learned as little as 30 percent of the curriculum measured on the test. In other words, the student does not know 70 percent of the curriculum deemed important.

Conclusion

In summary, certification examinations should be designed so that students who pass the test are proficient in each of the essential skills and knowledge expected of students at that level. Examinations should consist of subtests that measure each of the important skills; each subtest should have a sufficient number of items; and relatively high passing scores should be set for each core subtest. In this way, policymakers, educators, parents, students, and the community can be more confident in decisions about students' proficiency.

Notes

[1]Kellaghan (1993) reports that the following countries operate national assessment systems that also include measures of student achievements:

Australia, Canada, Chile, Costa Rica, Egypt, Finland, France, the Netherlands, New Zealand, the United Kingdom, and the United States. Lesotho and Uganda are in the process of establishing systems. (Ghana and Namibia have been conducting national assessments of student learning at the primary level for several years. The particularly poor performance of students in Ghana has attracted a great deal of attention and has sparked a national planning and reform effort to improve the quality of teaching and learning.

CHAPTER 3

Testing for Better Teaching and Learning

There are several ways to improve the quality of tests and test items so that they promote students' use of knowledge and encourage the development of higher order thinking and problem-solving abilities. Some of the strategies for improving tests and test items are to

- engage students in applying what they have learned to new situations,

- engage students in restructuring knowledge,

- encourage creative thinking,

- measure students' understanding of patterns and relationships,

- encourage experiential learning,

- measure ideas and concepts that provide students with explanatory power, and

- engage students in real-life contexts and tasks.

This chapter reviews the various ways that test items can be designed to promote better teaching and learning.

Using Appropriate Test-Item Formats

There are two general categories of test-item types: constructed-response items and se-lected-response items. Constructed-response test items ask the student to create or construct a response. These items are found on essay tests, for which the student prepares a written response, and on performance tasks, for which the student performs a complex task, such as giving a speech or designing an experiment. Selected-response items, or questions, provide several response options to the student, and the student selects from among the options, such as for multiple-choice, matching, or true-false items. Each format has advantages and disadvantages, and often there are trade-offs between the types of items or tasks that are more likely to encourage better teaching and learning and those that are more efficient and less costly to administer and score. In this chapter three types of test-item formats are reviewed, and examples of each type are provided. These formats are performance tasks, portfolios, and objective item, such as multiple-choice questions.

Why Should Policymakers Know About Item Formats?

Although knowledge about the different types of test-item formats may appear to be important only to test developers, it is also important to policymakers. Many measurement experts are technically skilled but not well informed about what constitutes good teaching and learning. Some tend to be more concerned with the statistical properties of tests than with their impact on teaching and learning. In part, this has contributed to the current state of testing in some countries in which technically correct tests have a negative and undesired impact on teaching and learning.

Another reason policymakers may want to know about the types of item formats is that the development, administration, and scoring of different types of test items have fiscal implications. It will cost far less to administer and score multiple-choice tests than performance tasks or essays—but multiple-choice tests are more likely to have a detrimental impact on the quality of teaching and learning. Conversely, well-designed performance tasks or essays are more costly to administer and score but can have a beneficial effect on teaching and learning. For policymakers to advocate the use of more costly approaches to testing, it is necessary to understand why they may be worth the extra expense.

Although this chapter is focused on performance tasks and portfolios, it does not mean that these are the only types of test items recommended. It is economically and administratively not feasible to have an entire public examination comprised of these types of tasks. The purpose in introducing them is to show how they can be used strategically to enhance the quality of teaching and learning. Each type of item or task has advantages and disadvantages, and examinations should include some of each. In reading the examples of various types of items or task formats in this chapter, it is important to consider the students and to imagine how the various types of questions can either enhance or detract from learning—how various approaches can make learning fun, interesting, and stimulating, or can make learning tedious, boring, and unimaginative.

Performance Tasks

For many types of performance tasks, the student actually *performs* with knowledge, rather than merely recalling or recognizing knowledge. A performance is a complex and important whole activity for which the student practices (for example, by collecting a sample of rocks and classifying them, or by interviewing family and community members about a topic and presenting the findings in a report). Performance tasks usually consist of several subtasks and often are not clearly structured; for example, a task may not necessarily be worded "First do this... then do that." However, a task may require that students clarify a problem, use their own judgment, plan, use trial and error, and often produce a tangible product.

Advantages

The primary benefit of performance tasks is that they require students to integrate a variety of skills, concepts, and knowledge and apply these to real-life situations. Performance tasks also tend to be more interesting and motivating for students and can make learning engaging. A recent study found clear academic benefits to making children want to attend to tasks: the study showed that the strongest predictor of increased test scores in mathematics was children's engagement with given tasks (Denvir & Brown, 1986). The reason for using performance tasks in a testing situation is to encourage teachers to use similar types of activities in the classroom to engage students in learning.

Disadvantages

Performance tasks are time consuming, costly, and complex to administer and score. They also tend to be limited in the breadth or scope of content they assess, although rich performance tasks can capture a student's depth of understanding. Because of these constraints, it is likely that their use in examinations will be somewhat limited.

Although it may not be feasible for some countries to use performance tasks in national examinations, it may be possible to use them in national assessments because only a small sample of students take the tests. To increase the likelihood that the tasks used in national assessments will influence teaching and learning, it is necessary to provide teachers with samples of similar tasks and notify them that such tasks will be used in the forthcoming national assessment. Although only a sample of schools and classrooms are asked to complete the tasks, it is best not to indicate which schools will be involved until the last minute so that all are engaged in preparing for the test. In this way the administrative and scoring costs are reduced, but the policy goal of encouraging teachers to teach using active learning through performance tasks is accomplished.

The introduction of performance tasks into the testing system is likely to require that teachers be provided with additional training and assistance in learning how to teach using such tasks. Therefore, there should *not* be consequences or sanctions associated with performance tasks until they have been used on an experimental basis and until sufficient support has been provided to teachers. Until that time, performance tasks can be used to try to influence instruction and to provide feedback to teachers, administrators, and policymakers.

Experimenting with performance tasks may require that educational researchers observe classrooms and interview teachers to find out how they are addressing instruction in performance tasks. If the researchers identify difficulties, then assistance may need to be provided to teachers. These difficulties should be expected, but they can be solved over time and the result will be more intellectually invigorated teaching and learning.

Care also must be taken to provide teachers and students with explicit guidance regarding what will be expected—what will be tested and how it will be tested. The "what" and "how" should be examples that illustrate the broader concepts, skills, and knowledge to be tested, such as in the reading and writing task in Figure 6. Teachers could be given a task like this as a model and told that it is similar to the types of tasks that will be on the examination. They should be encouraged to have students read a wide range of stories and to answer questions and have discussions about the stories that are similar to those in Figure 6. If teachers are told that the examination will measure (1) whether students really understand what they have read, (2) whether they are able to connect what they have read to what they already know or feel, and (3) whether they are able to express their

FIGURE 6

Sample Performance Task for Primary-Level Integrated English Language Arts

Getting Ready to Read

Here is some information about the story you will read. It will help you understand what is happening:

Little Willy and his dog Searchlight are in a dog sled race. So are Stone Fox and his five beautiful Samoyeds (a strong breed of dog with a thick white coat). The prize in the race is $500.

Little Willy hopes to win the money to save his grandfather's farm. His grandfather is very ill. Stone Fox hopes to win the $500 to buy back land for his Indian tribe, the Shoshone.

Reading the Story (Excerpt from *Stone Fox* by John Reynolds Gardiner)

This part of the story begins in the middle of the race. Read to see what happens.

As they approached the farmhouse, Little Willy though he saw someone in Grandfather's bedroom window. It was difficult to see with only one good eye. The someone was a man. With a full beard.

It couldn't be. But it was! It was Grandfather!

Little Willy was so excited he couldn't think straight. He started to stop the sled, but Grandfather indicated no, waving him on. "Of course," Little Willy said to himself. "I must finish the race. I haven't won yet."

"Go, Searchlight!" Little Willy shrieked.

"Go, girl!"

Grandfather was better. Tears of joy rolled down Little Willy's smiling face. Everything was going to be all right.

And then Stone Fox made his move.

He went from fifth place to fourth. Then to third. Then to second.

Until only Little Willy remained.

The lead Samoyed passed Little Willy and pulled up even with Searchlight. Then it was a nose ahead. Then the Samoyed regained the lead. Then Searchlight poured on the steam.

The crowd cheered madly when they saw Little Willy come into view at the far end of Main Street, and even more madly when they saw Stone Fox was right on his tail.

"Go, Searchlight! Go!" Little Willy cried.

Searchlight gave it everything she had.

She was a hundred feet from the finish line when her heart burst. She died instantly. There was no suffering.

The sled and Little Willy tumbled over her, slid along the snow for a while, then came to a stop about ten feet from the finish line.

The crowd became deathly silent.

Stone Fox brought his sled to a stop alongside Little Willy. He stood tall in the icy wind and looked down at the young challenger, and at the dog that lay limp in his arms.

(continued)

FIGURE 6 *(continued)*

"Is she dead, Mr. Stone Fox? Is she dead?" Little Willy asked looking up at Stone Fox with his one good eye.

Stone Fox knelt down and put a hand on Searchlight's chest. He felt no heartbeat. He looked at Little Willy and the boy understood.

Little Willy squeezed Searchlight with all his might. "You did real good, girl. Real good. I am proud of you. You rest now. Just rest." Little Willy began to brush the snow off Searchlight's back.

Stone Fox stood up slowly.

No one spoke. No one moved. All eyes were on the Indian, the one called Stone Fox, the one who had never lost a race, and who now had another victory within his grasp.

But Stone Fox did nothing.

He just stood there. Like a mountain.

After You Have Read the Story

1. This is only part of the story *Stone Fox*. After reading this part, what questions do you have about the story?
2. What feelings do you have about the story?
3. How do you think the story will end?
4. Choose a line from the story that you especially liked. Write the line here.
   Why did you choose this line?
5. Read these lines from the story again:
   Little Willy squeezed Searchlight with all his might. "You did good, girl. Real good. I am proud of you. You rest now. Just rest."

If you could look into the mind of Little Willy, what thoughts would you see? Draw or write the thoughts inside his head.

Working with Your Group

1. In your group, talk about the story you read. How did Little Willy feel about Searchlight? Below write what your group thinks.
   My group thinks that _____
   _____

2. The story you read showed how a young boy felt about his dog. By yourself, think about a pet you have or wish you could have. Draw this pet in the box below.

Now, write words around your drawing to describe your pet and your feelings about your pet.

(continued)

FIGURE 6 (continued)

3. In your group, share your drawing and words. Other members of your group may use words that you like. You may add these words to your drawing.
4. By yourself, cluster or list the things you like to do with your pet.
5. Share your cluster or list with your group.
6. By yourself, write a poem about your pet or a pet you wish you could have.
7. In your group, take turns reading your poems. As each person reads, listen for a word, line, or idea that you especially like.
8. After listening to everybody read, share what you liked about each person's poem.
9. What new ideas for writing about your pet did you get from your group?

Writing
Getting Ready to Write
   You are going to write about a pet you have or wish you had. What makes this pet special to you? What does it look like? What does it like to do? How do you feel about this pet? You may use your notes and drawing from your group work. You may use the space below to add any ideas as you get ready to write.

Time to Write
   Write about a pet you have or wish you had. When you write, be sure to include words that will help your reader "see" the pet you have or the pet you wish you had. Write as much as you can so that your readers will know all about this pet.

Reflecting on Your Reading and Writing
The teachers who will read your test want to know how you read and write. They are interested in what helps you understand what you read. Anything you want to say about your work on this test will be helpful to them.

1. What helps you understand what you read?
2. How did working in your group help you understand the reading?
3. How did working in your group help you get ready to write?
4. How do you think you did on this test?

From *A Sampler of English-Language Arts Assessment: Elementary, Preliminary Edition* (California Assessment Program), produced by the California State Department of Education, 1992, Sacramento. Adapted by permission. Text excerpt from *Stone Fox* copyright 1980 by John Reynolds Gardiner.

understanding in coherent writing, then teachers will focus on these objectives in instruction. It would do little good for them to have students memorize the facts of a story.

Language Arts Performance Tasks

During the past 15 to 20 years, significant advances in the teaching of reading and writing have influenced the design of curricula and tests. Earlier views of reading focused primarily on having the learner master a series of sequential and hierarchical skills. However, research has found that a reader must interact mentally with the text if he or she is to understand the material. Simply being able to sound out the words and read sentences and paragraphs aloud does not constitute reading. Most people have experienced reading a page without having any idea what they just read. When this is done, the reader is not engaging with the text and does not understand what was read. Strategies that contribute to effective reading include trying to predict what the passage will be about, asking questions when reading, and summarizing what has been read. In addition, a good reader monitors his or her attention. If the reader catches his mind wandering, he regains attention and rereads the missed text.

This more recent view of teaching reading focuses on four dimensions of reading:

1. how the reader builds meaning from print;

2. what the reader brings to the situation in terms of experience, knowledge, skills, and motivation;

3. how the information is presented in written text; and

4. the effect context has on reading.

New tests have been and are being developed to assess reading in ways that are consistent with this view of how students learn to read and comprehend. Several education agencies also are integrating tests of reading with tests of writing, and some are testing over several days rather than at one time. In some cases, students' process skills are activated during the assessment. For example, in reading, students may be asked to reread, make marginal notes, underline, list, cluster, comment, or predict what they think the text will be about—all skills that research has shown are used by good readers.

In writing assignments, students sometimes are asked to provide evidence of their growing understanding of the text and to incorporate their experiences and prior knowledge. Students may even be asked to reflect on their own writing processes, thought patterns, or the strategies and procedures they are using.

In the writing portions of integrated tests, the instructions may orient students to the type of writing they are being asked to do, focus their thinking, and help them anticipate the problems they must solve. The writing tasks establish both the purpose and context for writing by linking the writing task to earlier reading activities. Some education agencies are experimenting with several variations on this theme, sometimes preceding reading with writing; involving students in group discussions of their reading, writing, and editing; or having them write about their interpretations of subject-matter texts (see also Chapter 4 on essay tests).

Figure 6, mentioned earlier, is an example of an integrated reading and writing performance task for primary-level students. Appendix B contains additional examples of performance tasks. When reviewing these performance tasks, it is important to notice how

■ the tasks are designed to connect the story or poem to the students' existing knowledge, thoughts, and ideas;

- the students' thoughts and ideas are viewed as credible and important;

- prompts such as "My thoughts about what I am reading" help students see that reading is a process of making meaning that emerges as the reader progresses through the text;

- students are made aware of what they understand and do not understand by discussing the passage or story in small groups and sharing with one another their ideas about the meaning of the story; and

- students are encouraged to think about their own reading processes when they are asked, "What helps you understand what you read?"

It is also important to imagine how classroom teaching might change if teachers were given examples like the performance tasks in Figure 6 and Appendix B to prepare students for an examination.

Performance tasks and open-ended questions can involve students in restructuring information rather than simply recalling it—in explaining "why" and "how" rather than just "what." © Aga Khan Foundation/Jean-Luc Ray. Used by permission.

Science Performance Tasks

Many education agencies are beginning to use performance tasks to measure students' understanding of the process of science. Science is about discovery, and students need to understand that process. Unfortunately, most instruction in science at the primary level tends to focus on having students read from their texts and memorize scientific terminology. To encourage teachers to involve students in hands-on science tasks—actually doing science—a science test should include tasks that allow students to demonstrate their skills in laboratory techniques and in using scientific thinking processes. For example, students at the primary level can learn to classify and observe—two essential elements of the scientific process. Hands-on science tests that examine these skills might involve students in putting seeds and beans into categories and explaining why they selected those categories; or they might ask students to measure and record various objects, such as their pulse rate before and after exercise.

Primary-level science activities do not require a formal laboratory or expensive equipment. One primary school in Jamaica, located in a low-income neighborhood, used the tree in the school yard as a laboratory. The teachers had students bring jars from home to collect specimens from the tree. The specimens included insects, insect eggs, small plants, and fungi growing on the tree. The children returned to the classroom to observe, classify, and record their specimens. This inexpensive and easy assignment engaged students in experimenting with science as scientists would. Observing, classify-ing, and recording are the foundations of the scientific process and important activities for primary school children.

Hands-on science assessment is likely to be the most costly and complex form of performance testing, but it is probably the most essential. Many primary teachers are deficient in their understanding of science and may avoid teaching science at all. Evidence has shown repeatedly that if students do not learn to like science by the end of primary school, they will probably never like it. If hands-on science is not tested, it will probably not be taught.

Figure 7 contains a sample performance task in science for use at the primary level. Also included are background notes and guidelines for scoring the tasks that were provided to teachers. Appendix B contains another science performance task on measuring skills.

Mathematics Performance Tasks

In mathematics, there is now a greater focus on students' understanding of mathematical processes and on engaging students in real-life problem solving. The focus is on mathematical concepts that students develop over several years rather than in one month or one year. The goal is for all students to develop mathematical power—the power to do purposeful and worthwhile mathematical work.

Performance tasks are sometimes used to measure student learning in mathematics. They present students with a problem and ask them to respond by describing in writing their thinking and what strategies they are using to solve the problem. Students can be

FIGURE 7

Sample Performance Task for Grade 6 Science: Identifying Rocks

Information for Teachers

Objective: To assess a student's ability to test and identify the properties of a given set of objects (rocks) and then use this information to compare and infer the identity of an unknown object.

Materials:

Bag A	Bag B
1 Bag labeled "rock 1"	1 Bag labeled "rock 3"
1 Bag labeled "rock 2"	1 Bag labeled "rock 4"

(Note: Rock 1 is pumice, 2 is gneiss, 3 is calcite, and 4 is sandstone.)

2 plastic 9-ounce cups—one labeled "water" the other labeled "vinegar"
1 hand lens
1 plastic spoon
1 class-size bottle of vinegar

Not in kit: paper towels, white nail polish, permanent markers, and two plastic cups—one labeled "water" and one labeled "vinegar"

Background notes: Rocks are classified by how they are formed within the rock cycle, which is the cycle of deposition, formation, and erosion. Rocks that were once in liquid form within the earth (igneous) can be brought to the surface and cooled (volcanic) or hardened within the earth (plutonic). Rocks that are formed on the earth's surface are made by water, wind, and ice into sediments. Both igneous and sedimentary rocks can be buried and affected by heat and pressure of the earth so that their physical structure and chemical arrangement are changed (metamorphism).

This performance task encourages students to engage in inferential thinking. Inferences involve orderly, connected thinking. Using the inferring process, students learn that the conclusion of an argument is an explicit statement of something that is implicit in the premises. Its validity or consistency can be certified by logical considerations alone. To think well, students need experience in tracing their thoughts to their sources and then determining the truth of the source in order to judge its validity.

(continued)

FIGURE 7 *(continued)*

Science Performance Task

Directions: You are a geology student. Your teacher has asked you to investigate the properties of some rocks you found on a field trip.

1. In front of you are three rocks, "1," "2," and "3." You will need to perform four tests on each rock. Use the materials on the table to answer the following questions. Record your answers on the chart below.
    - Does the rock have holes?
    - Does the rock fizz when you gently place it in vinegar? (Leave each rock in vinegar for at least 30 seconds.)
    - Does the rock sink or float when you put it in water?
    - Does the rock have bands or stripes?

	Holes or no holes	Reaction to vinegar: Fizz or no fizz	Sink or float	Stripes or no stripes
Rock 1				
Rock 2				
Rock 3				

2. You may use the following information to help you name rocks 1, 2, and 3.
    Pumice—has holes, does not fizz, sometimes floats, has no stripes
    Calcite—has no holes, usually fizzes, sinks, has no stripes
    Gneiss—has no holes, does not fizz, sinks, has stripes

    Rock 1 is _____
    Rock 2 is _____
    Rock 3 is _____

3. In Bag B you have a mystery rock labeled "4." You will need to perform the same four tests on rock 4. Take the rock out of its bag. Do the four tests on the rock. Record your answers on the chart below. Put the rock back in its bag. Use the materials on the table to answer the following questions.
    - Does the rock have holes?
    - Does the rock fizz when you gently place it in vinegar? (Leave each rock in vinegar for at least 30 seconds.)
    - Does the rock sink or float when you put it in water?
    - Does the rock have bands or stripes?

	Holes or no holes	Reaction to vinegar: Fizz or no fizz	Sink or float	Stripes or no stripes
Rock 4				

(continued)

FIGURE 7 *(continued)*

4. Which rock is mystery rock 4 like? Check one box.
   ☐ Rock 1   ☐ Rock 2   ☐ Rock 3

Explain your answer based on the results of your tests.

Scoring Guide for Sample Performance Task for Grade 6 Science: Identifying Rocks

Outstanding...Rating = 4
> Gives conclusions—everything explained; conclusions match observations; gives clear justifications; explains answers based on tested and observed characteristics; uses examples; completes entire task.

Competent...Rating = 3
> Gives conclusions, but conclusions are not fully developed; conclusions match observations but have faulty justifications; gives faulty observations but good conclusions; supporting evidence on questions 3 and 4 is fair; completes most of task.

Satisfactory...Rating = 2
> Gives no conclusions, but attempts to explain are reasonable; provides some observations; offers weak explanations; completes second chart inferences based on data; completes part of task.

Serious flaws...Rating = 1
> Attempts to explain, but explanations do not make sense; responses are vague; unable to follow directions; completes very small portion of task.

No attempt...Rating = 0

Acceptable answers for a rating of 4 or 3 might include the following:

1. Rock 4 is like rock 3. It doesn't have holes or stripes and it sinks. (The idea is clear that the student made a decision based on the fact that these rocks have similar characteristics.)

2. It is calcite because I eliminated all other options.

3. The mystery rock is the same as rock 3 because it has the same characteristics.

4. It wasn't any of the rocks because it didn't match my characteristics of the other rocks. (This answer takes into consideration the idea that materials may have been faulty.)

From *New Directions in Science Assessment* (California Assessment Program), produced by the California State Department of Education, 1990, Sacramento. Reprinted by permission.

given from 15 to 45 minutes to respond and, in some cases, are allowed to use calculators or manipulatives, such as blocks or rulers. Such assessments ask students to

- restructure information rather than simply recall and reproduce it;
- understand and use information in new and unfamiliar contexts;
- explain why and how rather than just state a result of some arithmetic or algebraic manipulation;
- integrate and connect their conceptual understanding as they observe, reason, experiment, interpret, make decisions, and draw conclusions in situations they encounter within and outside of school;
- demonstrate persistence, imagination, and creativity; and
- approach problems in novel ways.

For example, rather than testing whether a primary-level student knows how to add or divide, a performance task might require that students survey members of their neighborhood about their smoking habits, present their results in the form of graphs or tables, and write interpretations or conclusions based on the survey data. This type of problem allows students to use various strategies to arrive at a solution and to present several possible correct solutions, depending on their assumptions. In one field test of this problem, students arrived at more than 60 correct interpretations or conclusions about the data. Figure 8 contains two examples of mathematics performance tasks.

The benefits of such tasks are that they provide the following.

- an interesting situation that engages students and involves mathematical concepts;
- multiple entry points that allow students at many levels of understanding to begin working on the problem;
- multiple solutions that allow students to make their own assumptions and develop creative responses; and
- usually a specific audience that creates the need for students to communicate effectively, using appropriate tools such as charts, graphs, and diagrams.

Portfolios

Assessment portfolios are planned selections of student work collected from work done throughout the school year. Portfolios include products that reflect a student's development over time. A portfolio differs from a student folder in that it contains a carefully chosen sample of student work rather than a collection of all the work. The portfolio serves four important purposes; it allows

1. teachers to assess the growth of students' understanding of a subject;
2. students to keep a record of their achievement and progress for self-assessment;
3. teachers and parents to communicate about students' work; and
4. opportunities for teachers to collaborate with other teachers to reflect on their instructional program.

At first glance, the power of portfolios may not be apparent, but several aspects of this

FIGURE 8

Sample Performance Tasks for Primary-Level Mathematics

Task 1 Train Ride

In this problem students must
- identify important elements of the problem, such as various denominations of money;
- explore possible combinations that yield 50 rupees and determine that all possible combinations have been accounted for;
- show combinations by using illustrations, tables, or charts; and
- organize the information so that it is most helpful to the friend.

A friend of yours, who just moved to India, must ride the train to her aunt's house each week. The train ride costs 50 rupees. Your friend must have exact notes and must use only 1-, 5-, and 10-rupee notes.

Your friend does not yet understand India's money, and does not know how to count India's money.

Help your friend find the right rupee notes to give to the fare collector. Draw and write something on a whole sheet of paper that can help her. She needs to see which combinations of rupee notes can be used to pay for the 50-rupee train ride.

Be sure to organize your paper so it is clear and helpful for your friend.

Task 2 Survey of Smoking

In this problem the students must
- analyze and interpret the data;
- draw conclusions from the data; and
- communicate their interpretations and conclusions to their peers in a style consistent with the style of the school newspaper.

The social studies class of Mombako Elementary School surveyed 100 of the school's 800 students about their smoking habits. The results of the survey follow:

38	never smoked
11	current smoker who has smoked less than one year
24	current smoker who has smoked more than one year
18	quit smoking less than one year ago
9	quit smoking more than one year ago
100	total

Write a short article that could appear in a school newspaper about the results of the survey. Include five statements that show interpretations or conclusions you derive from the survey data.

From *A Sampler of Mathematics Assessment* (California Assessment Program), produced by the California State Department of Education, 1991, Sacramento. Adapted by permission.

assessment process have potentially profound effects on students' inclinations to reflect on their own learning and academic development over time

Assessment is typically the work of teachers; students only respond to assessment. However, in using a portfolio a student can look at his or her work produced over a semester or a year and see what has developed, how it developed, where difficulties remain, and directions for future work. Students have access to the full scope of their work—a body of work that few students ever study. When using portfolios, students will no longer do their assignments and forget about them. Where portfolios are being used, students are beginning to talk seriously to one another about their "pieces of work" and to rely on their own judgments of quality.

Parents also can be involved in reviewing and selecting student work for inclusion in the portfolio. Some students have reported, "My mother learned more about the way I think." "My parents now know that I do take my work seriously and that I can be creative sometimes." "The thing that surprised me most is that she really liked it."

Students can be asked to think about their own styles—what improves with time, what needs work, and what has been forgotten. In treating their own work as they might the works of an established writer, painter, or musician, students confront fundamental questions concerning skill, insight, creation, and personal voice. As part of the process of reflecting on the body of their work, students can become aware of the particular signature they give to what they produce. This kind of self-awareness is a critical ingredient in students' ability to reflect on their learning.

Teacher involvement in selecting work for students' portfolios nurtures teachers' growth as readers and interpreters of qualitative, developmental information about their students. A teacher can engage in a dialogue with individual students about what work should be included and why it should be included. Guidelines can be prepared to help teachers understand each student's development and foster students' awareness of their own growth.

Groups of teachers and test developers will need to make decisions, such as the following, about how the portfolios are developed:

- What kind of structure will the portfolios have?
- What will go into them?
- How and when will the items be selected?
- How will the portfolios be evaluated or scored?

The decision about what should be included in a portfolio depends on questions about intended audience and what the audience might want to know regarding the student's learning, about the relations among items in a portfolio and other measures such as test scores, about how to best document progress toward identified goals, or about whether to include more than finished pieces. Portfolios can also include a record of student reflection and self-evaluation, which is done at various times during the year.

Several educational and testing agencies are experimenting with portfolios, and they are attempting to develop a scoring procedure that would permit the assignment of numerical scores based on the qualitative data contained in the portfolio. For example, what criteria would be used to assign one student's portfolio a 6 and another's a 10? Or one an A and another a C? Being able to assign some type of score makes it easier to judge the adequacy of a student's learning.

One of the primary benefits of using portfolios is the professional development of teachers that is promoted. After students and teachers work together at the classroom level to select work for inclusion in the portfolios, teachers work together at the school level to select the best from among those produced at each grade. The process moves through the administrative levels to district, regional, state/provincial, and national levels, with groups of teachers (and community members, parents, and researchers) examining, discussing, and finally selecting the best portfolios. At each stage, those involved engage in discussions of standards, excellence, quality, and purpose. When using portfolios to judge student work for school-based decisions, such as assigning grades or promoting a student to the next level, the review process does not need to extend beyond the school nor does a student's work need to be compared with that of other students.

A few U.S. state education agencies are attempting to develop portfolio-based assessments as the primary means of evaluating students and holding schools accountable. The decision to use this approach is based on the assumption that every teacher and student will be involved in determining the assessment activities and will be responsible for evaluating the activities. This approach requires training for teachers in articulating the standards for assessment activities and in evaluating their students' products in a manner consistent with other teachers. The role of the state is to establish the standards and to serve as an auditor. In that role, the state determines that the scores assigned to portfolios are accurate and that portfolios reflect actual learning.

There are several disadvantages to using portfolios. Teachers must devote extra time and work to their development, maintenance, and evaluation. Also, if portfolios are mandated by a government agency that declares that the portfolio must contain certain types of work, they can narrow the curriculum and instruction.

Objective-Item Types

An objective item, or question, is one for which the scoring is not open to interpretation. Although objective items can be written in different formats (such as true-false and matching), multiple-choice items are the focus in this chapter. (True-false items generally are not recommended because students will have a 50 percent chance of guessing the answer correctly.)

Multiple-Choice Items

With multiple-choice items, the test taker *selects* the correct answer from among several options—typically options "a" through "d." Selected-response items are contrasted with constructed-response items in which the student *constructs* a response by either writing, speaking, or perhaps creating a piece of art or music. Short-answer items are constructed-response items but generally require only a word, phrase, or sentence. Performance tasks and essay tests (described in the next chapter) also are examples of constructed-response item types, but they require longer responses. Following is an example of a multiple-choice item and a short-answer item.

Example of a Multiple-Choice Item

To fly from Cairo to Jakarta, the most direct route would be:

a. due east

b. due south

c. north, then west

d. east, then south

Example of a Short-Answer Item

To fly the most direct route from Cairo to Jakarta, which direction would you travel?

The choice between selected- and constructed-response item types can have a dramatic effect on what happens in the classroom. If the examination primarily contains items that ask students to select from among options, students are likely to spend much of their time preparing for the test with drill sheets in which they select the correct answer. Chapter 1 explained how this type of behavior is less likely to help students create the extensive web of mental connections that help them understand and use what they learn in school.

Advantages

Multiple-choice items have several advantages over constructed-response items:

1. Because multiple-choice items take very little time to answer and score, a test can measure a broader range of content than is possible with a test that relies solely on essay items or performance tasks.

2. They are less costly to score. If specially prepared forms are used, they can be machine scored, allowing thousands of answer sheets to be scored in a short time by fewer staff.

3. They are an efficient way to measure recall of factual knowledge and some skills.

4. Cheating is easier to detect on multiple-choice items through the use of computer programs designed for this purpose.

Disadvantages

The following list identifies the main disadvantages with using multiple-choice items:

1. It is more difficult to design multiple-choice items that measure higher levels of thinking and problem solving.

2. It is more difficult to design items that measure more complex, real-life types of skills and thinking.

3. Multiple-choice items take more time to develop because of the need to construct four or five response choices.

4. Multiple-choice tests promote multiple-choice teaching—memorizing the one, right answer.

5. There is a high chance of students' being able to get the correct answer by guessing, which is not the case with performance tasks or essays. If a multiple-choice item has four options, the

student has a 25 percent chance of guessing the item correctly; if only three response options are provided, the student has a 33 percent chance of guessing the item correctly.

6. It is easier for students to cheat on a multiple-choice test.

Although it is more difficult to measure higher order thinking using multiple-choice items, testing agencies have been experimenting with multiple-choice items that are believed to measure higher levels of thinking. In the multiple-choice questions in Figure 9, all are related to a single, broad top-

---

FIGURE 9

Sample Thematic Multiple-Choice Science Questions for Secondary Level

1. Juana and Paola planted 24 corn seeds and 24 bean seeds in soil containing a mixture of granite and organic matter. After planting the seeds in a sunny location, they watered them well with rainwater but noticed that the water did not immediately soak into the ground. When the seeds sprouted, Juana and Paola collected data and constructed a graph of the sprouting rates of the corn and bean seeds, shown below.

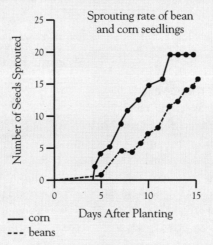

They also made the following observations about the seedlings:
- Corn seedlings had only one leaf. The veins in the leaves were parallel to each other.
- Bean seedlings had two leaves. The veins in the leaves were branched, and the two halves of the original seed were attached to the main stem.

Three weeks after the seedlings sprouted, they died. Juana and Paola tested the rainwater and found that it had a pH of 5.

(continued)

FIGURE 9 *(continued)*

1. Which one of the following is true about the seedlings?
   a. Both the corn and bean seedlings are dicots.
   b. Both the corn and bean seedlings are monocots.
   c. The corn seedlings are monocots, and the beans are dicots.
   d. The corn seedlings are dicots, and the beans are monocots.

2. The soil that Juana and Paola used probably came from
   a. the "A" horizon, or topsoil.
   b. the "B" horizon, or subsoil.
   c. the "C" horizon, or weathered rock.
   d. bedrock.

3. The water did not soak into the ground because
   a. the soil contained too much sand.
   b. the soil had a low permeability.
   c. the soil had too many pore spaces.
   d. the soil had good drainage.

4. Juana and Paola knew than corn and bean plants will grow better when the pH of the irrigation water is around 7. The rainwater they were using is
   a. neutral.
   b. acidic.
   c. alkaline (basic).
   d. saline.

5. According to the graph they constructed, how many bean seedlings had sprouted at 10 days?
   a. 8
   b. 10
   c. 13
   d. 15

6. Based on the data they collected, which one of the following is true about this experiment?
   a. Corn seeds grow better than bean seeds.
   b. Corn seeds need more water than bean seeds.
   c. Bean seeds need higher temperatures to sprout.
   d. More corn seeds sprouted than bean seeds.

From *California Assessment Program Field Test Collection: Working Materials*, produced by the California State Department of Education, 1991, Sacramento. Reprinted by permission.

ic and to one another. The questions assess students' understanding of not only scientific and agricultural facts, but also the thematic and conceptual underpinnings that serve as the framework for relevant knowledge and skills that are acquired, remembered, assessed, and used. Questions asked in this way are also more likely to promote learning through doing projects.

Costs

It is clear that performance tasks and portfolios will increase the cost of the testing program. However, the increase should be considered in light of the effect that such tasks may have on instruction: if tests energize rather than undermine quality learning in the classroom, the overall cost effectiveness is probably greater.

In addition, several education systems are involving teachers in developing and marking performance tasks and portfolios, and these teachers claim that it is the best staff development they have experienced. Thus, some of the funds allocated to staff development could be incorporated legitimately into the testing budget.

A Final Word

Each of the types of testing formats described in this chapter has advantages and disadvantages for use in the design of an examination or assessment system. Multiple-choice items can measure a large body of content knowledge fairly quickly and easily although generally at a lower level of thinking. Performance tasks and portfolios may encourage teachers to engage in more productive teaching behaviors.

In the next chapter essay tests are addressed. Ways to design and mark (score) these tests to promote improved teaching and learning are described.

CHAPTER 4
Essay Tests

Essay tests are superior to multiple-choice tests for measuring students' ability to synthesize, organize, and analyze subject-matter knowledge, and they are the most appropriate and direct way to measure writing competence. However, essay tests require more time to mark, or score, and are less objective than multiple-choice tests.

Because essay tests are less objective, there is a far greater risk that the marks that students receive on these tests, and the decisions made based on those marks, will not be valid or reliable. Therefore, it is very important that technical care be taken in developing, marking, and using essay tests. There are several ways that essay tests can be improved to contribute to better teaching and learning and to be more valid and reliable, including writing detailed specifications, writing prompts that clearly define the student's task, preparing test marking guidelines, and training markers and marking in groups.

These methods will be discussed in detail after the next section, which describes recent efforts to design essay tests that are aimed at improving writing instruction.

Testing to Improve Writing Instruction

Over the past several years, there have been a number of advances in strategies aimed at improving the teaching and testing of writing abilities. Most of these advances are in response to the research on teaching and learning described in Chapter 1, and they emphasize (1) teaching and testing different types of writing; (2) integrating reading and writing; and (3) prompting students to access and use the reading and writing-process skills that are known to increase students' ability to understand and remember what they learn.

Teaching and Testing Different Types of Writing

One important trend in the testing of student writing is the recognition that there are many different types of writing and that students should learn and be tested on a variety of types. Following are descriptions of some of the more common types of writing that are now being tested and taught (California State Department of Education, 1990c).

- *Autobiographical writing.* The writer tells about a specific occurrence in his or her life, writing vividly about the incident and stating or implying the significance of the incident to the writer.

- *Evaluating.* The writer makes judgments about the worth of an item, such as a policy, book, movie, or consumer product. The judgments should be supported with reasons and evidence.

- *Problem solving.* The writer analyzes a specific problem and suggests ways to solve the problem. Suggested strategies for solving the problem should be supported with arguments.

- *Reporting information.* The writer objectively presents data collected from observations or research to explain a phenomenon or concept.

- *Story writing.* The writer tells a fictional story with a plot, characters, dialogue, and scene.

- *Observational writing.* The writer describes his or her perceptions of an experience. The writer's view is that of an observer rather than that of a participant, as in autobiographical incident writing.

- *Speculating about causes or effects.* The writer presents his or her views about the causes or results of an event, trend, or phenomenon.

- *Reflective essay writing.* The writer explores an idea from different perspectives while reflecting his or her own thoughts and ideas. The writer demonstrates actual thinking that occurs while the piece is being written, considering a specific occasion, reflecting on it, and then generalizing to the world, in search of meaning.

- *Interpreting.* The writer interprets a text or data, providing reasons and evidence for the interpretations.

Each of these types of writing is useful in different professions and real-life situations.

For example, autobiographical and observational writing may be useful in writing letters to friends or relatives or in writing stories. Evaluating, problem solving, and reporting information are essential for stimulating students' analytical abilities and preparing students for the type of writing they will do in secondary school, at university level, and in many jobs. For example, a scientist must be able to write an accurate, unbiased report of information; a journalist must be able to write observations of incidents or experiences; and all individuals should learn to think about the connections between cause and effect and how to analyze and solve problems.

If these types of writing are tested, they are more likely to be taught. In addition, the process of writing specifications and scoring criteria (described later in this book) dictates that the specific requirements for each type of writing be articulated, which can facilitate the teaching of each type of writing.

Teachers who have marked essay tests that measure these various types of writing have expressed their growing appreciation and understanding of the importance of teaching and testing different types of writing. Here are selected comments from teachers who have been involved in the marking sessions (California State Department of Education, 1990b):

> "The reflective essay is a powerful way to tie personal and general views to either a student's own life or his or her reading of literature. It fills that void in high school where personal writing almost disappears, and it encourages students to move beyond a restricted sense of self and see how their 18 years of experience reflect other people's experience."

"Have students concentrate on an incident and magnify that incident. Tell students to freeze a moment in time, take the reader there, and help him see that moment, feel it, touch it, really experience it."

"Students need frequent practice in defining reasonable arguments on both sides of a controversial issue and in giving evidence to support both stands."

"I will ask students [in small groups] to read the scoring guides and then to create appropriate prompts and responses."

"This can't be prepared for a week ahead of the test, and it is not the responsibility of the English teacher alone. Writing as a process should be taught year round and across the curriculum."

Integrating Reading and Writing

In some integrated reading and writing tests, students are asked to provide evidence of their understanding of a text and to incorporate their own experiences and prior knowledge. This approach is based on research that has found that the reader builds meaning from print by connecting his or her experience, knowledge, skills, and motivation to the information presented in a text. Having students write about what they read encourages them to absorb, integrate, and think more deeply about what they are reading.

For example, one integrated reading and writing test has primary-level students read a poem selected specifically for young children. After they have read the poem, they are asked to respond to several prompts in writing, such as, "Explain how you are alike or different from the child in the poem" or "If you could have a conversation with the child in the poem, how would it go? Write the conversa-

tion you might have" or "How did this poem give you a new understanding of a child who may be very different from you?" These types of questions are cognitively multifaceted; they encourage children to analyze the poem, articulate what they know about themselves, compare and contrast themselves to the child in the poem, write dialogue, be creative, and try to understand something from someone else's viewpoint. These questions also recognize the student as a valuable source of information, experience, and opinions and are more likely to motivate and engage children. If teachers believe that students will be asked such questions, they will incorporate them into their teaching.

Other types of integrated reading and writing tests measure students' ability to interact with and analyze sophisticated subject matter with social and policy implications. For example, one test, developed for use at the secondary level, has students read several historical documents and answer questions regarding the issue of freedom of the press, which include having them analyze legal cases related to libel and freedom of the press. Some of the questions ask, "Explain the case against the defendant. What are the arguments on each side?" "What is your decision on this case? Explain your reasons."

There are various ways that reading and writing are being integrated for measurement purposes, including preceding reading with writing; involving students in group discussions of their reading, writing, and editing; or having them write about their interpretations of subject-matter texts. (See Figure 6 in Chapter 3 for an example of an integrated reading and writing test.) The processes used to read and write have been found to be important and to distinguish fluent readers and writers from poor readers and writers. Addressing these process skills also has become a focus in modern testing strategies.

Prompting Students to Use Their Reading and Writing Process Skills

A recent trend has been to integrate process skills that help students understand what they are reading. Making marginal notes, underlining, listing, clustering, commenting, or predicting what the text will be about are skills that research has shown are used by good readers. Recently developed tests activate such process skills within the body of the test. In these tests students often are told that they may refer to the reading passage as often as they like and mark it up in any way that will help them develop their understanding of the passage. This teaches children that they may need to read something several times to understand what the author is trying to convey. This is particularly essential when students are reading complex material such as textbooks and when they are reading to prepare reports or research papers. Research has found that poor readers tend to believe that if they cannot understand something the first time they read it, they will never be able to understand it. Some students need to be taught these reading strategies to help them increase their understanding of the text.

Students also may be prompted to *reflect* on their reading processes within the test. For example, they may be asked, "What helped you understand what you were reading?" or "How did working in your group help

you get ready to write?" The purpose of this reflective approach is to measure skills and knowledge in a way that is consistent with good teaching and learning.

Research on the Testing of Student Writing

One organization specializing in research on testing, the National Center for Research on Evaluation, Standards, and Student Testing (CRESST) located at the University of California at Los Angeles, studied students' written explanations of history and science content for five years (Baker et al., 1992). CRESST developed a model derived from the cognitive research summarized in Chapter 1 for assessing students' deep understanding of subject-matter content. The model addresses the following dimensions:

- activate students' prior knowledge in the content area being measured;
- have students read primary source documents that contain new information; and
- have students write an explanation of important issues that integrates new and prior information.

The test developed by CRESST begins by having students answer a 20-item, short-answer quiz with questions designed to measure students' knowledge of historical principles and events that are relevant to the history writing task (see Figure 10). Students then read opposing viewpoints in primary source text materials, such as historical speeches and letters, and respond to a prompt that sets their writing task within a context.

FIGURE 10

Test of Students' Prior Knowledge

How Much Do You Know About U.S. History?

Directions: This is a list of terms related to U.S. history. Most of them are related to the Civil War period, but some of them are from other periods in U.S. history.

In the space after each term, write what comes to mind when you think of that term *in the context of U.S. history*. A brief definition or a brief explanation of why that person, place, or thing was important is acceptable. If the term is general, such as "civil rights," give both a general definition and a specific example of how the term fits into U.S. history.

Good example: civil rights—Rights guaranteed to all citizens regardless of race, sex, religion, etc. Blacks fought for their civil rights in the 1960s. Martin Luther King, Montgomery bus boycott.

Do not define the term by simply restating the same words.
Bad example: survival of the fittest—Only the fittest survive.

Even if you are not sure about your answer, but think you know something, feel free to guess. There are probably more items here than you will be able to answer in the time given. Start with the ones you know best, and work quickly so that you can answer as many as possible. Then go back and answer the ones of which you are less sure. Do not spend too much time on one specific item.

List of Terms Related to U.S. History

1. Popular sovereignty _____
2. Dred Scott _____
3. Communism _____
4. Missouri Compromise_____
5. Industrialization _____
6. Gold Rush _____
7. Bleeding Kansas _____
8. States' rights _____
9. Federalism _____

[Note: The complete prior knowledge test typically contains 20 items.]

From the *National Center for Research on Evaluation, Standards, and Student Testing (CRESST) Performance Assessment Models: Assessing Content Area Explanations* (CSE Technical Report Series), by E.L. Baker et al., 1992, Los Angeles, CA: CRESST. © 1992 by The Regents of the University of California and supported under the Office of Educational Research and Improvement, U.S. Department of Education. Adapted by permission.

(Prompts are explained in detail later in this chapter.) They are asked to write an essay that explains the positions of the authors of the texts and to draw on their own background knowledge for explanation.

The marking criteria for the test are arranged into six scales used to judge student performance (see Appendix D for examples of marking guides):

1. *General impression of content quality*— How well does the student know and understand the historical content?

2. *Use of prior, relevant knowledge*—How well does the student incorporate concrete facts, information, and events that are not provided in the texts supplied to elaborate his or her position?

3. *Number of principles or concepts*—How many different social studies concepts or principles does the student correctly use?

4. *Argumentation*—How well does the student organize historical knowledge to make a convincing and logical argument?

5. *Use of text*—How well does the student use information from the text for elaboration?

6. *Number of misconceptions*—How many misunderstandings in the student's interpretation of the text and historical period are there in the essay? What is the scope of the misunderstandings?

CRESST researchers have field tested the essay test model and have demonstrated the reliability, validity, and generalizability of the technique. The model is documented fully in a handbook (Baker et al., 1992) that includes sample tests, specifications, scoring criteria, and detailed instructions for training markers to use the marking criteria for judging students' essays. The CRESST researchers believe that this assessment strategy can be useful for performing large-scale assessments and for providing diagnostic information to improve instruction, although different types of reports would need to be prepared for the different audiences. In addition, the types of writing tasks that the CRESST researchers have developed can be used in various ways, such as during a class period, as a homework assignment, for a longer paper, or even by students working cooperatively in small groups or pairs. The most unusual aspect of the CRESST assessment model is its attempt to activate and measure students' prior knowledge, as mentioned earlier.

These various approaches to measuring writing proficiency may help improve the teaching of writing and can show teachers how to make writing assignments more engaging and motivating for students. They also can expand the range of types of writing that are taught in schools.

Increasing the Validity and Reliability of Essay Tests

There are four components involved in developing a high-quality test using essay-type items and performance tasks: (1) writing detailed specifications, (2) writing clear prompts, (3) preparing marking criteria, and (4) training markers and marking in groups. Incorporating each of these components will reduce the subjectivity and increase the validity, reliability, and comparability of the test items and the decisions that are made using students' responses to them. As discussed previously, validity means that the test measures what is intended and that appropriate decisions are made based on the test results. Reliability means that the test is consistent: all students interpret the question in the same way that was intended by the test developers, all test markers score using the same criteria, and all teachers interpret the test results in the same way. Comparability means that the test scores can be compared across students, schools, or classrooms.

All testing is concerned with the variability in students' abilities as represented by the test scores, but variability can be determined reliably only if all other factors are constant. Detailed specifications, explicit prompts, marking guides, trained markers, and group scoring all help reduce unintended variability and ensure consistency in the decisions made based on the essay test results.

Component 1: Writing Detailed Specifications

As described in Chapter 7, specifications define both the content and the behavior to be measured. The content includes the facts, knowledge, concepts, or principles of the subject matter to be tested; the behavior defines the procedures, strategies, or solutions the student will apply, such as compare and contrast, define, or list. The specifications also define the type of writing or skills to be measured and the audience to which the writing is aimed.

Figures 11, 12, and 13 are specifications for an essay test intended for secondary students using history text materials as the subject matter about which students are expected to write. Figure 11 lists specifications for the essay test; Figure 12 specifies the types of history text materials that may be used in the test; and Figure 13 gives specifications for the prior knowledge component of the task (which is shown in Figure 10). When reading these specifications, it is important to think about the implications they have for teaching students to prepare for an essay test.

Although specifications written for essay tests and performance tasks will require a different format from those described in Chapter 7, the purpose is the same—to define and delimit what is being tested and how it is being tested.

Component 2: Writing Clear Prompts

The prompt is the information that is given to the students to direct them to write or perform the task. It tells students what to write about, how long the writing sample should be, and who the audience is, and it may specify other criteria by which the students will be judged. The prompt also indicates how much time students will have to complete their response. (Note: recent research indicates that students should be given sufficient time to engage in all the desired stages of the writing process—planning, writing, reviewing, and revising.)

Sample prompts that are written with and without sufficient guidance for students are shown in Figure 14. Notice that the first prompt is much more specific in telling students what is expected of them. These expectations should be articulated in the specifications upon which this and other, similar prompts are based. In addition, the scoring guidelines described in the next section

FIGURE 11

Essay Task Specifications Using History Text Materials

Essay context	Students should be given a historical context to frame the written response, consisting at minimum of a time, historical period, and occupational role.
Audience	The audience for the students' writing is specified to be a particular person in the same target historical period. The person must be ignorant of the information provided in the texts for some plausible reason, such as living abroad or returning from a long trip, to heighten the verisimilitude of the task.
Intellectual task	Students need to prepare an explanation of the dispute or topic included in the text selection(s). This explanation requires the students understand the viewpoints expressed, compare and contrast perspectives using inference strategies, and synthesize the explanation referring to both relevant text material and prior knowledge.
Directions	Students should be given the directions that state the context and audience and cue them to critical format issues. The directions must underscore the need to use knowledge the students have acquired about history outside the text as well from the provided texts.
Administration	Directions can be printed at the top of sufficient paper for writing provided to the students. Students can also construct their answers using word-processing equipment.
	Students should have the text selections available to them as they write.
	Students may be asked to complete the task in one class period (approximately 45 minutes), or they may be given a chance to revise their work. In the latter case, students should turn in their work at the close of each period.
Scoring scheme	Essays should be scored in terms of the six scoring dimensions described at length in the training materials [listed earlier in Chapter 4].

[Note: A prompt written to these specifications is in Figure 14.]

FIGURE 12

Specifications for History Text Materials

Topic	Must be a regular and significant part of the secondary school history curriculum.
	Must provide an issue that has implications beyond the particular historical period.
Text structure	Must provide for contrasting views, explanations or contexts.
	May use either a single piece or short contrasting pieces.
	May be written in narrative or expository form.
	Must be written so that esoteric or technical discussions are minimal, special vocabulary is limited, and the author's viewpoint is clear.
Text source	Must use primary source materials. Accepted pieces include letters, transcripts of speeches, editorials, and excerpts from documents.
	As a rule, provide only two major text selections. However, supplementary materials, including written personal reactions by historical figures, maps, songs, and other relevant material, may be made available if adequate time is provided for the students to understand the materials. The students may be told that these materials are "required" or "optional."
	Editing of materials should be avoided except to excerpt sections from the longer piece.

From the *National Center for Research on Evaluation, Standards, and Student Testing* (CRESST) *Performance Assessment Models: Assessing Content Area Explanations* (CSE Technical Report Series), by E.L. Baker et al., 1992, Los Angeles, CA: CRESST. © 1992 by The Regents of the University of California and supported under the Office of Educational Research and Improvement, U.S. Department of Education. Reprinted by permission.

should be consistent with both the specifications and the prompt. Together, these components produce a highly systematic, integrated, and coherent writing assessment—one that articulates the dimensions of writing to be tested and to be taught and learned.

Component 3: Preparing Marking Criteria

Marking criteria are the guidelines, or criteria, used to score students' responses to the prompt on the essay test. They should be prepared by those responsible for developing the

FIGURE 13

Specifications for the Prior Knowledge Measure

The prior knowledge test [example shown in Figure 10] involves the use of a 20-item, short-answer assessment. The purposes of this measure are to activate students' relevant prior knowledge for subsequent application in the essay, measure their relevant prior knowledge in the subject matter, and get a general assessment of students' knowledge of U.S. history. Both broad principles and specific facts are measured.

Stimulus format	Proper names, terms, numbers, and short sentences provided to students should not exceed 8 words for each item.
Forms of knowledge	The items listed for students should consist of specific facts, events, dates, quotations, and the names of principles or concepts.
Distribution	Half the items should reference specific information, such as an event, and half the items should reference concepts (for example, federalism) or principles (constitutionality). At least two-thirds of the items should relate to the immediate historic period of the assessment (plus or minus 10 years of the date or dates of the text). The remaining one-third of the items can precede or follow the period under assessment.
Directions	Students should be encouraged to respond rapidly and to write the essence of their understanding briefly. There are no requirements for form, such as writing in complete sentences.
Administration	Approximately 20 items can be provided in a 10- to 15-minute period.
Marking scheme	Responses are scored on a five-point scale (0=low; 4=high). Students are given a "4" if they write an accurate, elaborated definition, description, or context for the stimulus term; a "3" if they are essentially correct; a "2" if they have some incomplete notion of the term; a "1" if they have no idea; and a "0" of they make no response.

From the *National Center for Research on Evaluation, Standards, and Student Testing* (CRESST) *Performance Assessment Models: Assessing Content Area Explanations* (CSE Technical Report Series), by E.L. Baker et al., 1992, Los Angeles, CA: CRESST. © 1992 by The Regents of the University of California and supported under the Office of Educational Research and Improvement, U.S. Department of Education. Reprinted by permission.

FIGURE 14

Sample Writing Prompts

Example of an Adequate Prompt
History Writing Prompt
   Remember 12 June 1964, when, at age 12, you and your father arrived early at the Rivonia Trial courtroom to catch a glimpse of seven black South Africans on trial for treason. You watched as Nelson Mandela denounced state-supported discrimination against blacks and vowed to "take up again, the struggle as best I can…." You watched as he was pronounced guilty of treason and given a sentence of life in prison.
   Now, 29 years after that historic trial, you have house guests visiting from Australia. The son of your guest asks you to explain this "struggle" and why a man convicted of crimes against the state has been seen on television shaking hands with the President of the United States.
   Write an essay in which you explain the most important ideas and issues your guest's son should understand. Your essay should be based on two sources: the general concepts and specific facts you know about South African history, especially what you know about apartheid and what you learned from yesterday's readings. Be sure to show the relations among your ideas and facts.

[*Note: Students were provided with the text of a speech by Nelson Mandela and an article from a South African newspaper that reported on the history of the African National Congress and the Rivonia Trial.*]

Example of an Inadequate Prompt
Write a paragraph on one of the following:
a. an apple
b. a good deed
c. the computer

test at the time the test is written. Why should marking criteria be prepared? Without specified criteria, one test marker may judge a student's writing using different criteria from other markers. For example, one marker may place great emphasis on neatness in handwriting and proper punctuation; another may be looking for a creative response; another may be concerned with determining that the student learned the facts or content covered in the course; another might judge whether the student uses relevant examples or symbolism; and yet another may be concerned with all these criteria. If the markers arrive at different marks for a student's essay, then their marks are variable—they vary from one marker to another. Without marking criteria, it is likely that if one marker rates a student's examination, the student might pass, and if another marker rates the same examination, the student might fail. Such variability renders unreliable what may be an otherwise good test—and reliability is an essential criteria of a good test. Marking guidelines are essential for ensuring consistency in marking and for making valid decisions based on students' performance on the test.

Sometimes brief marking criteria are prepared but may not be sufficiently detailed to prevent unintended variability in individual markers' scores. For example, the marking criteria prepared for one essay item on an examination for grade 8 students are as follows:

> Attempts of less than 13/14 sentences will not be given more than 33 percent credit. Deduct half a mark (about) for each wrong spelling. Incorrect tense should not be given any credit. Assess the subject matter carefully. [*Students were not told in the examination that their responses should be of any particular length—so they are being judged by criteria of which they are not aware.*]

Although these criteria are somewhat specific, especially with regard to the length of the composition, spelling, and tense, the direction to "assess the subject matter carefully" is vague and could lead to considerable variability in the marks assigned by different raters. In addition, the criteria do not address other important aspects of writing such as developing and supporting a position, presenting the information in a logical and consistent manner, writing for a particular audience, or using language choices that enhance the text.

Marking criteria should represent standards endorsed by experts knowledgeable in the subject area and should relate to those features of content and written expression that are amenable to instruction. For example, "richness," "depth," or "vividness," may be desirable features in an essay, but unless educators can demonstrate that they can teach such qualities, they should not be evaluated on a test.

Types of marking systems. There are several approaches used to evaluate students' writing, but the two most frequently used are holistic and analytic. The holistic approach makes judgments about the overall quality of the essay and has the advantage of requiring less time to mark. However, it generally does not provide much feedback for instructional improvement. The analytic approach requires separate judgments for various aspects of the essay, such as quality of the ideas, spelling, and mechanics, and it is more likely to provide guidance for instructional improvement. (A sample of a holistic and an analytic marking guide is in Appendix D.)

An early version of a marking system developed by the California State Department of Education (1990c) Assessment Program used a three-part guide. Each essay was marked on rhetorical effectiveness, general features, and conventions. These parts are described as follows:

1. *Rhetorical effectiveness* judges whether the student has addressed the specific requirements for the type of writing being assessed. For example, in evaluative writing the writer should state and support his or her judgment about something, such as a book or product. In writing about a controversial issue, the writer should take a position and attempt to convince readers that the position is reasonable. Each type of writing has some-

what different requirements, and the rhetorical effectiveness criteria are tailored to that specific type of writing.

2. The *general features* scale is concerned with criteria that are common to all types of writing. These may include features such as coherence, style, or use of concrete language. The assessment may focus on only one or two of these general features each year, and those features that are selected for focus may be determined based on deficiencies in the previous years' results.

3. The *conventions* scale rates students on the conventions of writing, such as usage, grammar, mechanics (capitalization and punctuation), and spelling.

Whatever marking approach is used, the most important considerations for those concerned with improving the quality of teaching and learning is that the criteria are consistent with the aims of the assessment and with the instructional program. The criteria should result in a report of test results that can be used for instructional improvement at various levels. It is equally important to articulate criteria for evaluating students' writing about subject-matter content.

Component 4: Training Markers and Marking Essays in Groups

Those who mark essays should be trained to use the marking guides. Training helps ensure that all individuals marking essays are interpreting and applying the evaluation criteria in a uniform way. Bringing markers together to mark in groups and providing them with training will increase the reliability of the marking process.

Training markers has become somewhat standardized and involves introducing markers to the marking guides, allowing them to practice applying the criteria to a set of papers, and conducting a trainer-led discussion of the features of each paper that result in the paper's classification or grade. Generally two markers read and mark each paper. If there is disagreement, the paper is read by a third marker. Periodic checks help ensure that there is no misunderstanding in the interpretations of the criteria; if there is, additional discussions are held to clarify disagreements.

Marking as staff development. Marking often is conducted by groups of teachers and subject-matter experts. Using teachers as markers has the advantage of engaging teachers in discussions about what good writing (or performance) is and how they should be teaching. This practice has been found to result in substantial improvements in the teaching of writing and in significant increases in the amount of writing that students do in the classroom. However, some states or countries choose to contract the marking process to organizations that specialize in marking essays and performance tasks. Although this approach may result in somewhat greater reliability, it does not provide staff development benefits.

Marking in support of educational reform. If tests are to be used as tools for reform, all teachers ideally should be involved in marking. This is an important way to communicate quality work and to articulate standards. Although it may not be feasible to involve all teachers, it is a goal that is worth pursuing.

It may be useful to conduct a study for a two-year period to compare the behavior of teachers involved in marking with those not involved. If the evidence indicates that teachers involved in marking *do* change their behavior in positive ways, as has been found in other studies, the costs associated with this approach to improving educational quality should be weighed against the costs of other, more traditional approaches.

Individual marking—the path to inconsistency. A number of countries develop brief marking criteria and then give a stack of papers to individuals who do the marking in their offices or at home. This approach does not provide the benefit of discussing the criteria with other markers, and it is likely to result in a high degree of inconsistency in the marks and to contribute to incidences of cheating.

The handbook cited earlier, prepared by CRESST (Baker et al., 1992), contains detailed instructions for training markers and for conducting marking sessions. These instructions include who should mark, the number of markers needed, how training should be organized, a sample agenda for training and for marking sessions, a description of the trainer's responsibilities, how the room should be set up for training and marking, materials needed for training, materials needed for marking, training procedures to be followed, forms for use in calculating reliability of marking, marking procedures to be followed, how to report results, and a complete set of guidelines for each of the six marking scales described earlier.

Another approach to marking tests has been used in some African countries. The approach establishes several layers of responsibility and quality control in the marking process. It involves an experienced chief examiner who is responsible for marking a particular essay. This chief examiner is assisted by two or more assistant chief examiners and team leaders, who each supervise four to six other examiners. Using copies of representative scripts from previous exams, this team trains new examiners before the examination. After the exam has been administered, the chief examiner selects what he or she considers representative scripts marked by the other examiners. As marking progresses, these examiners check the reliability of the marking process and make appropriate corrections.

An important element of any approach to rating is that a detailed marking guide is prepared at the time the essay questions are developed. It is expected that the marking guide may be revised during the marking process, but marking criteria should be part of the thinking that helps define what is important for students to know and what is the best way to measure what they know.

A Final Word

Each of the aspects of testing using essay-type items and performance tasks, described in this chapter, is essential to ensuring that students are judged using a common set of criteria. Without specifications, clearly stated prompts, marking criteria, group marking and marker training, students will not understand clearly the purpose or focus of their performance; markers will judge students' responses using different criteria; and the test will not be a consistent or comparable measure of students' abilities.

CHAPTER 5

Integrating Examinations, Assessments, and Continuous Assessment

This chapter addresses the question of whether examinations can be used as national assessments and argues that, if examinations are revised to be more consistent with a criterion-referenced approach to testing, they can be used cost effectively for national assessment purposes. Although it may not be economically feasible for a country to implement examinations, national assessments, and a continuous assessment system all at once, whatever systems are instituted should be coordinated with one another and with curriculum and instruction. In addition, each of these testing systems is an opportunity to promote quality teaching and learning. Most countries already are operating examination systems, and testing reform can begin with improvements in these existing systems.

Testing at Different Levels of Complexity for Different Purposes

Each of the three types of measurement systems—examinations, national assessment, and continuous assessment—measures students' abilities at different levels of complexity. Examinations are administered at the end of a cycle (such as primary school or secondary school) and should measure whether students have learned to integrate and apply

the range of skills, knowledge, and concepts taught at each of the grades in the previous levels. Certification and selection examinations generally are *not* used to diagnose students' deficiencies because students will not be at the same school the following year to receive remedial assistance; detailed analyses of students' strengths and weaknesses are not needed in these tests.

One of the policy-level intentions of examinations should be to encourage teachers and students to use *combinations* of the skills and knowledge they have been learning throughout that particular educational cycle and to *apply* what they have learned to new and real-life situations. For example, at the primary level students should be able to read and interpret simple text and write coherently about that text. In mathematics, students should be able to perform the four basic calculations and know which operation to apply in real-life situations. Both of these are examples of the integration of numerous subskills that are taught throughout primary school. (See the performance tasks in Chapter 3 and the essay tests in Chapter 4 for other examples of tasks that integrate several subskills as applied in real-life contexts.)

There are several advantages to testing for certification and selection purposes using complex, integrated, and real-life tasks. The primary benefit is the positive impact on teaching and learning that these tasks have. A secondary benefit is that, because so many subskills are subsumed within a single task, the test can contain fewer questions. Another advantage is that real-life tasks are inherently interesting for students, so they are more likely to try harder, pay attention, and be engaged. Another benefit is the staff development involved if groups of teachers are brought together to mark the examinations. Finally, these sorts of integrated, applied items are similar to those needed by employers and in daily life.

Continuous assessments generally include both detailed tasks (such as word recognition in reading and place value in math) and larger, more complex and integrated tasks.

For national or regional assessments, it is also important to measure student learning in subskill areas as well as in integrated and applied skills. Both levels of information can be useful to teachers, principals, curriculum and textbook developers, inspectors, and teacher trainers for guiding instructional improvement efforts.

Can Examinations Be Used for National Assessment Purposes?

There is debate about whether examination results can be used for assessment purposes. It would be ideal if a country could operate examinations, continuous assessment, *and* a national assessment. However, if a country is unable to expend the funds for both examinations and a national assessment, there are ways in which examinations can be useful for national assessment purposes.

Using examinations for national assessment purposes means that all or part of the examination results are aggregated and reported at school, district, regional, and national levels, in addition to the individual student level. The examination results can be quite valuable to school staff and to regional- and national-level policymakers if they are provided in useful formats. (See Chapter 8 for a discussion of reporting and using test results.)

The problems with using examinations as national assessments are summarized in the next section. Following each problem is a suggestion for how the impediments might be overcome. These suggestions are offered as alternative ways to view the existing situation and not as proven solutions to the problem. They are offered in an attempt to alleviate some of the increased costs associated with multiple testing systems.

Problem 1: Examinations Need to Use Items That Discriminate

Selection examinations are designed to discriminate between high- and low-scoring students. To ensure discrimination, items that most students answer correctly or that most do not answer correctly are removed from the test, as mentioned earlier. This means that a selection examination is not likely to accurately reflect the whole curriculum, and it will not be an appropriate measure for reflecting those achievements mastered by most students. An assessment is intended to find out what students know and do not know, so it should accurately reflect the curriculum and students' achievement.

Possible solution. Because selection examinations have such a profound influence on what is taught and learned in classrooms, a different conception of selection examinations may be needed if they are to be considered useful for national assessment purposes. Until recently, selection examinations were viewed solely as tools for selection. It is now acknowledged that they also influence teaching and learning. Selection examinations should be redesigned to do both—aid selection and positively influence teaching and learning.

It may be possible to redesign selection examinations to support these goals and still allow for the discrimination needed to select those students who are most likely to perform well at higher levels of learning. It can be assumed that a country's primary and secondary curricula were selected because the skills and knowledge contained in them are important preparation for learning at subsequent levels of education (although the curriculum also may include practical subjects aimed specifically at those students who do not continue their schooling). Therefore, it follows that the skills and knowledge contained in the curriculum are what students need to be well prepared for higher learning, and students who do well on measures of the curriculum are the ones most likely to do well at higher levels of learning. The selection examination therefore should measure the curriculum of

Examinations should be designed to aid selection decisions and to positively influence teaching and learning. © Aga Khan Foundation/Jean-Luc Ray. Used by permission.

the prior level of learning. This ensures that the curriculum gets taught and that students and teachers are not forced to divide their time between preparing for the selection exam and studying the curriculum—they will be the same.

Will an examination that measures the curriculum provide the range in examinee performance to allow selection of a few "best" students? First, because developing countries are faced with severe limitations in the resources available to produce a high-quality education system, it may be years before large numbers of students are able to master the complete primary curriculum and to perform exceptionally well on selection examinations.

Second, the difficulty level of the examination can be manipulated if it appears that there are more students qualifying for selection than there are places available. Here is how that situation might work: Examinations can measure what is in the curriculum, but the difficulty and complexity of the examination can be increased by adding items or tasks that require students to combine and apply specific skills and knowledge to novel situations. These more complex, difficult items should provide the needed range in examinee scores. Students who successfully respond to the more complex items or tasks are more likely to adapt to the learning demands of higher education. The more complex questions could count only for selection purposes, whereas the questions measuring the more basic skills and knowledge would count for certification. Both sets of questions could be analyzed and reported for national assessment purposes because both would provide useful information to policymakers and other educators.

Problem 2: Too Many Subjects Are Tested

Although both examinations and national assessments may be concerned with measuring student performance in core skills, such as basic literacy, numeracy, and reasoning skills, most examinations also measure several other subjects. It is not unusual to find tests offered in 20, 30, or more subject areas.

Possible solution. Although examinations may measure student learning in several subject areas, aggregation and reporting of results could be limited to the areas of interest for national assessment policy purposes (such as reading, writing, and mathematics).

Problem 3: There Is Insufficient Quality Control in Marking of Examinations

Marking procedures for examinations generally are not clearly specified and rely heavily on the judgments of individual markers.

Possible solution. The topic of standardizing the marking of examinations is addressed in detail in Chapter 4 on essay testing. That chapter explains how to prepare marking guidelines, how to train markers, and the importance of marking in groups rather than individually. These strategies can help improve examination systems regardless of whether they are used for national assessment purposes.

Problem 4: Students Are Allowed to Choose Subjects or Questions

Students are often allowed to choose the subjects or questions they elect to answer in examinations. This means that not all students would respond to items used for the national assessment, which eliminates the possibility of making valid comparisons among students and schools. For example, if an examination has 100 questions and 20 of those questions offer students a choice of answering one of three options, students are responding to essentially different examinations. This precludes valid comparisons of student performance. If valid comparisons cannot be made, how can judgments be made indicating that one student is better than another and should be selected for entry into secondary school or university?

The issue of comparability is further complicated by a practice called "compensation," in which students are allowed credits in one curricular area to make up for a relatively poor performance in another area. In a World Bank study (Kellaghan & Greaney, 1992) the authors describe several examples of compensation. Ethiopian students who score poorly in Amharic, English, and mathematics can qualify for a certificate by moderate to good performance in political education, general science, and social science. Such a certificate would lose its meaning if it is supposed to indicate that these students are proficient in the core skills expected of a certain level of education.

In another example, in Togo, students who receive low scores on the written examination can compensate by taking an oral examination. A student in Lesotho who obtains a 90 percent in all subjects but one, in which he or she scores below 50 percent, would receive only a third-class pass; but a student who obtains at least 60 percent in English, Sesotho, and mathematics, and at least 60 percent on the examination as a whole,

would receive a first-class pass. Clearly, the student who scores 90 percent in all but one subject would be the better student but would receive a lower passing mark.

Together, the practices of compensation and allowing students to choose the questions they will answer undermine the validity of judgments that make comparisons among students possible.

Possible solution. An alternative approach that would provide comparability and yet allow flexibility on examinations is to establish standards in certain core skills and knowledge in which all students must demonstrate proficiency. The core skills should include reading, writing, numeracy, basic science, and reasoning. These are also the primary areas of interest for the purpose of a national assessment. Students could opt to take examinations in other subjects that could be recorded on their certificate.

Problem 5: Assessments Require Greater Depth of Coverage Than Examinations

National assessments may require more extensive coverage of the curriculum than is needed for a national certification or selection examination. National assessments tend to focus primarily on the core content areas of mathematics, language arts, and science but are concerned with assessing schools and students in the many topics within these areas. In addition, generally only one subject is measured each year, not all three subjects every year.

Possible solution. Because the concern in a national assessment is not with individual students, it is not necessary that every student answer every question. Matrix sampling is an approach in which all questions are answered by some students, but no question is answered by all students. In this way, if there are skills or knowledge for which national assessment data are desired but are not needed on the examination, they could be added to the examination but only answered by a sample of students. This would mean that each student would have only 5 to 10 extra questions on the examination, and these questions would not need to count toward certification or selection.

Problem 6: Examinations Are Designed to Compare Students

Marks on selection examinations are based on how a student compares with other students taking the examination, rather than what the student can or cannot do. For national assessments, the concern should be to describe what students know and can do.

Possible solution. Selection and certification examinations and national assessments all should be developed according to principles of criterion-referenced testing described earlier in this book. Norms can be established for criterion-referenced tests for use in making selection decisions or other types of comparisons. This approach allows the tests to be used to make comparisons *and* to report what students know and can do.

Problem 7: Assessments Require Midcycle Data

In conducting a national assessment, countries are typically interested in identifying the strengths and weaknesses in the education system at various levels. The belief is

that if there are problems in the system, they should be identified and remedied early rather than waiting until it is too late in a child's education. This suggests that national assessments may need to be administered in the middle of a cycle of schooling and perhaps again toward the end of the cycle. However, examinations usually are not administered until the end of a cycle.

Possible solution. A test could be administered only for purposes of national assessment during the primary cycle, perhaps at the third or fourth year of schooling. This test would not be used for selection or certification purposes. Although this is an instance of instituting a national assessment decoupled from an examination, it is still far less costly to administer an assessment at only one grade than to administer a national assessment at three or four levels of schooling.

Problem 8: Examination Takers Are Not Representative of School Population

Not all students are required to take examinations, especially selection examinations. This means that the data on student achievement would not necessarily reflect all students and, in fact, may be least representative of the lower achieving students who are less likely to sit for a selection exam. For a national assessment to reflect the status of teaching and learning for the entire system, it should include all students at the grade levels being tested.

Possible solutions. One option is to require that all students take certification examinations. This would also help reduce instances in which schools discourage slower students from taking the examinations in order to ensure a better reputation for the school. A school could be rated, in part, based on the number of students it is able to retain successfully from grade 1 through the end of primary school. The number of students taking the examination at the end of primary school could be compared with the number enrolled at grade 1 and with those taking the national assessment at grades 3 or 4.

Problem 9: There Are Changes in Examinations Over Time

There is a concern regarding the comparability of examinations over time because there are changes in passing scores and in test items from year to year.

Possible solution. A carefully developed test plan that specifies the content and skills that are to be measured can help ensure comparability of examinations from year to year. In addition, the specifications written to guide the development of items in a criterion-referenced approach also will permit a greater comparability in examinations over years. More detail on test plans and specifications is in Chapters 6 and 7.

Examinations *Can* Be Used for National Assessment Purposes

If a country has sufficient resources to implement both a national assessment system and examinations, many of the problems described in this chapter can be averted. However, many of these problems exist because the ways in which examinations are designed and used are inappropriate and should be improved. To review, the changes needed to use

examinations for national assessment purposes may include the following:

1. Ensure that selection examinations measure the skills and knowledge viewed as important to learn at the previous level of schooling.

2. Use a criterion-referenced testing approach for developing examinations and national assessments.

3. If it appears that more students are receiving high scores than can be selected for enrollment at the next level, the examination can be made more difficult by adding more complex items or tasks that measure the application and integration of skills and knowledge taught at the previous level,

4. Collect information and report results in a way that takes into account a school's background and contextual factors.

5. Add questions and tasks to examinations that measure students' higher level of thinking and problem-solving abilities.

6. Require that *all* students take examinations in core subjects and skills, and eliminate choice in the items to which they are allowed to respond. Take steps to ensure that the examinations students take are comparable.

7. Limit national assessments of student learning to one subject per year and begin assessing at the mid-primary level.

8. Require that all students sit for certification examinations and national assessments. Evaluate schools, in part, on

the proportion of their student body that sits for the examinations as compared with the proportion that entered grade 1.

9. Add a section to the examination and assessment regarding students' attitudes about learning and their classroom experience.

The next chapter describes the importance of preparing a plan for testing activity and how a test plan is prepared.

CHAPTER 6
Preparing a Test Plan

A test plan is a document that specifies the purpose of the test; who will use the results of the test; how the results will be used; the level of test results needed (such as individual student, school, district, or region); and the skills, knowledge, and concepts to be measured by the test. The test plan also addresses other issues, such as how long the test should take to administer; how many items it will contain; the types of items that will be on the test; and whether it will be machine scored, hand scored, or both.

Why Are Test Plans Important?

Writing a test plan, or test specifications (which differ from *item* specifications that describe in detail how the items, or questions, on the test will look), is a critical step in test development: if the plan is written properly, it helps ensure the success of the other steps in the process; if a test plan is not prepared, or if it is developed carelessly, it is likely that the test will not provide valid or reliable information. A test plan helps ensure that the test is appropriate for the intended purpose. For example, many curricula indicate that an aim of the instructional program is to have students learn knowledge and skills that they can apply in their everyday lives. However, when the end-of-cycle certification test is designed, the application of knowledge and skills often

is not measured. Another example is a national assessment that intends to measure basic English-language literacy but includes items that measure complex grammar, which is far beyond what is considered as basic literacy. In both cases, the tests do not measure what is intended.

A test plan also is useful for ensuring that the test is representative of the content and skills to be tested. For example, tests of writing ability sometimes measure only knowledge of grammar and punctuation but do not measure students' ability to write. The process of writing a test plan should cause test developers to think through more carefully these issues.

A test plan also is important in guiding the development of the test. To develop a test without a test plan would be like trying to build an office building without architectural blueprints. The test plan allows all those who are working on or using the test to have a common understanding of what the test is for, what it measures, and how it should be constructed.

A test plan also can be useful when selecting items from an item bank—a collection of test items—to construct alternative forms of the test.

How Is a Test Plan Prepared?

Although a teacher who gives a test or quiz in class would not need to prepare a test plan, tests given for broader purposes should begin with a plan. The higher the stakes associated with a test, the more important it is that a test plan be prepared. (See the introduction for an explanation of high-stakes tests.) The steps involved include the following.

Establish a Committee

A plan should be prepared by a group of individuals who represent various aspects of teaching and learning in the domain to be tested. These individuals could include classroom teachers, university faculty in the subject area, curriculum subject specialists, teacher trainers, those who conduct or are knowledgeable about research in the teaching and learning of the subject, and one or more testing specialists.

Decide on Purpose and Content

Careful thought and discussion should go into specifying the purpose of a test. What may seem obvious at first glance may involve many subtle implications. For example, if the purpose of the test is to select students for higher levels of learning, the committee should consider the evidence about the low predictive validity of most selection tests. In one study, Somerset (1965) calculated the correlation between students' performance on a selection examination and their performance four years later on a secondary school leaving examination. The correlations were very low, and there was almost no correlation among students who obtained just above a passing score on the selection examination and their end-of-school performance. This means that only some of the students who did well on the selection examination did well on

the secondary certification exam, and some of those who did poorly on the selection exam did well on the leaving exam. There is also evidence that selection examinations overpredict for boys and underpredict for girls. This means that qualified girls do not get selected and that boys get selected who do not perform well at the next level of schooling. These examples highlight the issue of test validity and emphasize that the test plan should address how the validity of the test will be determined.

Although the purpose of the test may be apparent, there are sometimes unintended outcomes that should be considered, such as the influence that a selection exam may have on teaching and learning as discussed throughout this book. The purpose of the test should be stated clearly with all extenuating issues detailed in the plan.

Establish Priorities

As with developing a curriculum, it is likely that many more topics will be selected for an examination than time or resources permit. This means that priorities need to be established and some of the topics omitted. One strategy for delimiting the test is to focus on broader, more complex and higher level skills and content when measuring for end-of-cycle purposes, and to include more subskills when measuring for ongoing performance when the test results will be used to help improve the teaching and learning process. Herman, Aschbacher, and Winters (1992) provide a list of questions to help categorize the priorities as follows:

■ What important cognitive skills do we want students to develop?

- What social and affective skills do we want students to develop?
- What metacognitive skills do we want students to develop?
- What types of problems do we want students to be able to solve?
- What concepts and principles do we want students to be able to apply?

Represent Content Domain

When preparing a test plan, it is important to make sure that the items on the test are representative of the content domain. The *domain* is the range of skills, knowledge, and concepts embodied within the intended subject or topic. A domain might include all the content covered in grade 4 mathematics or only part of a course, such as fractions or decimals. The size of the domain depends on the purpose of the test. For example, if a teacher gives students a quiz with 10 multiplication problems, the teacher is not interested merely in the students' status on those 10 items; rather, the teacher is using the students' performance on the quiz to indicate their overall mastery of multiplication. However, if the teacher is interested only in students' ability to multiply single-digit numbers but only includes items on the quiz that are 5 times another number, then the quiz is *not* representative of the domain of all single-digit numbers.

A traditional example of the domain of reading for grade 6 is provided in Figure 15. In this version, three main reading skills—vocabulary, comprehension, and study-locational skills—and the application of those skills to content areas have been selected. Within each of these main skill areas, several subskills

and sub-subskills are tested: for example, the subskills of comprehension include literal comprehension and inferential comprehension; understanding cause and effect is a sub-subskill of inferential comprehension. When preparing a test plan, designers need to determine which of these reading skills are appropriate for the test purpose and for the grade level of the students intended to take the test.

Prepare a Matrix

A matrix typically is used to help ensure that a test measures a representative sample of the subject domain and is representative of the range of cognitive levels. On the left side of the matrix are the skills or topics to be measured, and across the top of the matrix are the kinds of cognitive levels at which the skill or topic is to be measured, such as factual recall, comprehension, application, synthesis, or analysis. The cells in the matrix indicate the number of items to be used to measure the particular skill at the specified cognitive level. The matrix could be extended or another matrix prepared to indicate the types of items to be used (such as multiple choice, performance tasks, or essays), or to ensure that both genders are equally represented in the test items or that urban and rural populations are fairly represented. In addition, the more precise the list of the skill areas to be tested is, the more likely that the item writers will interpret accurately the intentions of the test designers. One version of a partial test matrix for the domain of reading (in Figure 15) is shown in Figure 16.

One important issue discussed earlier is whether the test (and test plan) should be developed to reflect the current curriculum

FIGURE 15

Skill Areas in Reading for Grade 6

I. Vocabulary
  A. Recognizing prefixes, roots, and suffixes
  B. Recognizing word meanings
  C. Using context with multiple-meaning words

II. Comprehension
  A. Literal
    1. Understanding details
      a. from a single sentence
      b. from two to three sentences
    2. Recognizing pronoun references
    3. Understanding sequence
  B. Inferential
    1. Determining main ideas
    2. Understanding cause and effect
    3. Following organization
    4. Putting information together
    5. Predicting outcomes
    6. Making comparisons and contrasts
    7. Drawing conclusions from details
    8. Drawing conclusions from overall meaning
  C. Interpretive
    1. Analyzing character
    2. Understanding setting
    3. Summarizing plot
    4. Understanding dialogue
    5. Sensing mood
    6. Understanding figurative language
  D. Critical/applicative
    1. Detecting author and author's attitude
    2. Detecting author's purpose
    3. Separating fact from opinion
    4. Applying knowledge to a different context

III. Study-locational skills
  A. Understanding reference material and parts of a book
  B. Interpreting maps, graphs, and charts

Reading in the Content Areas
I. Vocabulary—word meanings
  A. General
  B. In science
  C. In social studies

II. Comprehension of interpretive passages
  A. Literal
  B. Inferential
  C. Interpretive
  D. Critical/applicative

III. Comprehension of science passages
  A. Literal
  B. Inferential
  C. Critical/applicative

IV. Comprehension of social studies passages
  A. Literal
  B. Inferential
  C. Interpretive
  D. Critical/applicative

From *Reading Framework for California Public Schools: Kindergarten Through Grade 12*, produced by the California State Department of Education, 1980, Sacramento. Reprinted by permission.

FIGURE 16

Partial Matrix for the Skill Areas Assessed in Reading for Grade 6

Skill Area and Rationale	Number of Items	Descriptions of Skill Area	Illustrative Test Question
B. Inferential: The fullest comprehension requires rising above the literal to the inferential—to induction, deduction, analogy, and other logical processes. It also invites individualistic, imaginative elaborations based on what the writer has suggested. These sets of competencies are sometimes called "thinking skills." Although these competencies are not unique to the reading process, they are essential to success in reading.	127	The student will identify main ideas, associate causes and effect, follow organization, put information together, predict outcomes, make comparisons and contrasts, and draw conclusions from details and overall meaning.	See examples for each specific reporting category following.
1. Determining main ideas	16	The student will discriminate between the topic of a passage and lesser details within the passage or will recognize a paraphrase of the gist of the passage.	The main idea of this passage is that a. the wrasse is a fish that keeps other fish free of sores by cleaning them of parasites. b. a wrasse's cleaning station can be many things. c. the Pacific Ocean has many kinds of fish. d. the wrasse is a parasite that feeds off of other fish, causing sores to form. (See passage B.)

(continued)

FIGURE 16 (continued)

Skill Area and Rationale	Number of Items	Descriptions of Skill Area	Illustrative Test Question
C. Interpretive: Awareness of various levels of comprehension is of particular importance as the teacher formulates both oral and written questions. Classroom instruction historically has emphasized student responses at the literal level. Although this level provides the foundation for comprehension at higher levels, attempts should be made to expose students to activities and questions that stretch their thinking. Research indicates that the kinds of questions teachers ask and the way in which they ask them can influence student thought processing. Teachers who incorporate a variety of questions before and after the reading experience are actively involved in promoting thought and comprehension.	79	The student will analyze characters, infer setting, summarize plot, understand dialogue, sense mood, and interpret figurative language. Some of these skills (such as inferring setting and summarizing plot) apply exclusively to the literary passages. Items assessing character analysis, dialogue, mood, and figurative language do occur in several social science passages.	See examples for each specific reporting category following.
4. Understanding dialogue	12	The student will identify the message of quoted dialogue, the speaker of the quoted material, and/or the listener to whom it was directed.	You can tell that the wolf thought that a. the lace could be used in making a nest. b. the leg of the boot was the deep hole of a nest.

(continued)

FIGURE 16 (continued)

Skill Area and Rationale	Number of Items	Descriptions of Skill Area	Illustrative Test Question
			c. the bird's eggs could go on top of the boot. d. the birds could put the boot up in the tree. (See passage A.)
5. Sensing mood	12	The student will recognize the mood of an entire passage or of parts of a passage (such as the beginning or ending).	At the beginning of this story, the mood is one of a. disappointment and sorrow. b. curiosity and excitement. c. fear and suspense. d. thankfulness and joy. (See passage A.)
6. Understanding figurative language	12	The student will identify the meaning of a metaphor, simile, idiom, or other image or figure of speech used in a passage, story, or poem.	The author's choice of the words "sets up business" and "cleaning station" are used to show that a. the wrasse's means of getting food is almost like a business service. b. wrasse fishing is big business. c. all fish set up stations. d. the wrasse enjoys cleaning itself in the water. (See passage B.)

From *Reading Framework for California Public Schools: Kindergarten Through Grade 12*, produced by the California State Department of Education, 1980, Sacramento. Adapted by permission.

and instructional materials. For example, if one of the intentions of the test is to encourage teachers to teach at higher levels of thinking and challenge students' problem solving skills, and these skills are not currently specified in the curriculum, the test may lack curricular and instructional validity. If there are problems with the existing curriculum and textbooks, the development of a test to reflect these problems only will reinforce inappropriate teaching and learning. Ideally, the development of tests and instructional materials should be done at the same time, with test developers and curriculum developers working together. However, this opportunity is not always possible.

One way to measure content or skills different from the existing curriculum and to ensure validity on a test is to provide teachers (and perhaps students) with information about what will be on the test and to show them examples of the test items. The matrix sample for testing reading skills discussed earlier was prepared for this purpose; several other examples of ways to provide teachers with test information are provided in Appendix F. It is important to provide such information well in advance of giving the test to ensure that teachers and students have a reasonable amount of time to work on these skills. The amount of time needed may vary, depending on the purpose of the test: for example, if the test is to be used to select students for higher levels of schooling, then a considerable amount of time is needed—at least two years; but if the purpose of the test is to improve teaching and learning and to assess the effectiveness of schooling at regional levels, less advance notice is needed—as long as there

are no negative consequences such as punishments associated with the test results.

Consider Assessment Alternatives

In preparing a test plan, it is important to think about the various ways to test the skills and knowledge of interest. Each of the alternatives has advantages and disadvantages, which were discussed in Chapter 3 and are mentioned briefly here. For example, multiple-choice items are quick and easy to score and allow the test to cover a broad range of content. If many students are to be tested, a multiple-choice test can be efficient. However, if the aim of the test is to influence teachers to teach problem solving and higher order thinking and to provide students with more active learning experiences, it is appropriate to include performance tasks, open-ended questions, or essay items. These types of items may be less viable if a large number of students is taking the test because they require more time to administer and score. One option is to include some of each type of item—several multiple-choice items to cover more content and a few performance tasks and essays.

Consider Other Factors

Other factors that will need to be considered include the length of the test, the number of test forms needed, resources that may be needed to take the test (such as rulers, calculators, dictionaries, or materials for hands-on science tasks), the number of items on the test as a whole, and the number of items for each of the subtests. The issues of test-item tryouts and field testing are addressed in Chapter 9.

Review of the Test Plan

After the plan is developed, it should be reviewed by several appropriate individuals and revised accordingly. The test plan serves as the framework for guiding the development of the item specifications described in the next chapter. The test plan describes what the overall test will look like, and the item specifications describe what the test items or tasks will look like; both are important elements in the testing process.

CHAPTER 7

Item Specifications

Item specifications are detailed and precise descriptions of what will be measured on a test, how it will be measured, and the allowable content. Specifications are essential when preparing items for both examining and assessment purposes. Specifications help ensure that all items that measure a particular skill, concept, or knowledge measure it in comparable ways—ways that have been carefully considered in advance. The considerations will take into account factors such as students' developmental level, their life experiences (including cultural or regional backgrounds), the curriculum, the instructional materials, and common learning errors.

Why Are Specifications Important?

Specifications Help Ensure Test Validity

Specifications are prepared to ensure that what is measured is what is intended to be measured and that the measurement is not influenced by factors that are not intended. For example, in a multiple-choice test item some students may be able to eliminate several of the response options (correct and incorrect answers) because the options give unintended clues, as in the following items.

Select the word that means about the same as the word in capital letters.

1. SMART
   a. clever
   b. stupid
   c. unfortunate
   d. poor

2. GLOOMY
   a. happy
   b. somber
   c. luminous
   d. good

In these examples, students who do not know the correct answer might be able to *guess* the answer because the connotations of the incorrect words are all very different from the correct answer. That is, in the first item the words "stupid," "unfortunate," and "poor" all have a *negative* connotation, and "clever" stands out because it is the only word of the four options with a *positive* connotation. If a student knows that "smart" has a positive connotation, he or she can eliminate the other three words without knowing what they mean or what "smart" means. The same situation could occur in the second item with the word "gloomy" and the four options listed.

The items in these examples may not measure students' understanding of the intended words, but rather their understanding of connotations. These unintended factors can be controlled by writing specifications. For instance, the specifications for the earlier sample items could state that the incorrect response options must have the same connotation as the correct answer.

Here is another example of a test item that may not measure what is intended:

> Write in your own words (150 to 200 words) about any one of the following:
>
> a. It is a great virtue to be helpful.
>
> b. An apple falls to the ground.
>
> c. A computer.

In this item, from a secondary-level selection examination, it is unclear what is intended to be measured. The item presumably is related to the ability to communicate in writing, but it is not clear whether it asks for creative writing, expository writing, the ability to develop an idea and provide supporting details, punctuation or correct spelling, clarity, persuasiveness, or factual knowledge.

The process of writing specifications encourages those involved to think more clearly, deeply, and analytically about what they intend to measure and to explore various ways of measuring what is intended in relation to the possible effect on teaching and learning.

Specifications Serve as Guides for Item Writers

Specifications are used to tell item writers what content, skills, or knowledge will be measured and what the items should look like. This guidance is important to ensure consistency in the items measuring a skill. For example, in measuring primary school students' reading comprehension ability, a passage written at the grade 12 level would be much more difficult for students to understand than a passage written at the grade 3 level. Well-written specifications ensure that all passages are written at approximately the same level of difficulty so that there can be a common interpretation of scores across all students who take the test. Or, they may specify that a range of difficulty be included in the test so that each student's reading level can be determined.

Generating a collection of items that measure the same skill at approximately the same level of difficulty relates to the issue of reliability. Obtaining reliability, or consistency, across items measuring a skill is important. To estimate whether an individual student knows or can do something, repeated observations of the student's performance in that skill are necessary. Proficiency means being able to exhibit a behavior consistently—not sporadically. For example, if a soccer player can kick the ball into the goal only 1 out of every 20 times, he would not be recruited for the national team. However, if he can score a goal consistently 18 out of 20 times, he would be a terrific recruit for the team because the coach would be fairly confident that he is *proficient* in scoring goals. The same situation applies to students and learning: to be confident that a student is proficient in a skill, a teacher needs to know that the student can perform the behavior more than once—especially if the student performed well on only one multiple-choice question on which there is a fairly high chance of answering correctly just by guessing. Therefore, to obtain a reliable estimate of a student's proficiency in a skill or understanding of a topic, the student needs to answer several items that accurately measure the skill. The number of items needed will vary depending on how the skill is measured (for instance, more items are necessary for multiple-choice and fewer for constructed-response items such as performance tasks), how broad the skill or concept is, and how important the stakes are (for example, if the test is for selection purposes or diagnosis purposes).

Specifications Help in the Preparation of Item Banks

Item banks are collections of test questions or problems from which items can be drawn over time or across regions. A bank of items can be used to develop alternate forms of a test for use in subsequent test administrations. In this way, the same skills, concepts, and knowledge are tested from one year to the next, but different items are used each time (at least some of the items are different). Because different items are used each time, the chances of students' cheating are reduced. Using specifications to guide item-writing increases the likelihood that the collection of items written to measure a particular skill or concept measures what was intended.

Ensuring that tests are comparable from year to year is particularly important in a national assessment because one of the primary concerns of an assessment is to measure changes in the system over time. If a test measures different knowledge from one year to the next, it is not possible to make valid judgments about improvements or declines in student learning. This does not mean that new skills or measures cannot be added to

the assessment or that modifications cannot be made; rather, a core set of skills, concepts, and knowledge to be tested should remain constant over time.

There is an important caveat to remember about maintaining test items. Sometimes the items that compose an assessment instrument are so flawed that they should not be used. Two instances of primary-level national assessments come to mind. Both assessments contained items that were far too difficult for the level of students being measured. In one assessment, the reading passages were several grade levels above what is appropriate for a native-English speaker and were even less appropriate for students whose first language is not English. In the other national assessment, many of the items measuring English grammar were too difficult and were not appropriate skills to be taught at the primary level. When adult English speakers were shown the items, all were unsure of the correct answers and indicated that they were remote uses of English grammar. In both instances, the test makers noted that they had designed the tests to measure the local curriculum and textbook content. There is clearly a need for a careful review of the instructional materials and a change in the assessment instruments. It is neither valid nor worthwhile to continue measuring inappropriate skills and content simply to maintain a consistent test from year to year. An achievement test always should measure what is deemed important by the test makers for students to learn.

Although tests should be comparable from year to year, they should not be exactly the same. If the same test items are used each year, teachers may require students to memorize those items and may not focus on teaching more generalizable skills or the broader context of knowledge. Writing many items to a single specification allows test makers to sample from among the collection, or bank, of items to be used each year the test is given and to ensure that the same skills are measured each year.

Consistency is also important when groups of students or schools are compared. If a country uses regional testing boards and each board develops its own test, it is impossible to make valid comparisons regarding students' performance across regions. However, if one set of specifications is used and each region develops its own items to match those specifications, valid comparisons across the regions are more reasonable—assuming that the items written in each region are congruent with the specifications.[1]

Specifications Tell Teachers and Students What Is Important to Learn

Specifications can be used to communicate to teachers, students, teacher trainers, and other relevant audiences what will be tested and how it will be tested. However, a different format of specification is typically used for this purpose. Specifications written for teachers can influence teaching and learning and can help focus attention on generalizable skills and concepts rather than on memorization of specific test items found on previous tests.

Recently, there have been some major changes in how specifications are viewed. For the past 15 years or so, it was believed that when writing a criterion-referenced test to measure a particular skill, only *one way* of measuring the skill should be selected and the set of specifications should be written to describe that particular way. However, problems arose using this approach. It was observed that teachers taught the skill in this particular way *only*, and they neglected to teach it in the variety of other formats that are important for children to learn. Students often were not able to generalize the skill to other situations. For example, if a test measured subtraction horizontally (such as in this equation 56–42 = ___), teachers were more likely to teach only horizontal subtraction and to neglect to teach other forms or uses of subtraction.

To avoid this problem, Popham (1995) recommends that to communicate effectively with teachers about what is to be measured on a test, the descriptions should provide several generalizable ways to teach the skill rather than just one. The descriptions should articulate the *intellectual essence* of the skill, concept, or knowledge to be measured along with what is *eligible* to be tested (such as subtraction up to two decimal places). Although any given form of a test might sample only one or two of the eligible testing strategies, all the strategies listed in the specifications would be allowable. Appendix F contains several examples of communications with teachers about what is to be measured and what is important to teach.

What Do Specifications Look Like?

Specifications written for test-item writers are more detailed than those written for teachers. Measurement specialists disagree about the level of detail at which specifications should be written, and there is variation in the terms used to describe the parts of a specification. However, almost all specifications contain four essential parts:

1. an objective or general description of what is to be measured;

2. a sample test item that represents the skill to be measured and the way in which it will be measured;

3. a description, or set of rules, about how the problem, question, or task is to be stated; and

4. a description, or set of rules, about how the student is to respond.

Some specifications also may include a supplement that lists allowable words and documents, such as spelling words, cities and countries, or chemical equations. For example, the list of spelling words that would be allowable for students in grade 3 is different from that for students in grade 8. Each of the four parts of a test-item specification is described more fully in Figure 17.

Several samples of item specifications are shown in Figures 18, 19, and 20. In these sample specifications, it is important to notice that there is considerable variability in the level of detail provided. The specification in Figure 18 for measuring students' knowledge of how to alleviate the symptoms of nutritional deficiency is quite detailed; item writers are limited in the types of items they can write to match the specification. The advantage of this level of detail is that all the items written to this specification would be homogeneous—they would all measure the same skill in the same way and at the same level of difficulty. If several of these items are used on the test, the results would provide a fairly reliable estimate of each student's ability in this skill, as measured in this way.

The disadvantage of such strict specifications is that teachers are likely to teach this skill in only this one way, unless the specifications given to the teachers list some other ways to measure this skill.

Another sample specification shown in Figure 19 for writing test items that measure students' ability to classify objects is much less detailed and precise. There is quite a bit of variability in the kinds of items that can be written while keeping within the guidelines in the specification. However, it is possible that the items written would not be homogeneous, so they may not provide a reliable estimate of student ability.

In studying the sample specifications in Figures 18 and 19, it is important to consider the kind of detailed analyses that are required to write the specifications. Even for a specification for test items intended to measure a skill as simple as telling time (see Figure 20), the decisions are numerous and must be discussed and debated in light of what is reasonable for students to know, in terms of their age, grade, the curriculum, and textbooks used. For example, those writing the specifications must think through whether children at that age should know time to the hour, the half-hour, the minute, and so forth. They must consider the size and shape of the clocks that are likely to be seen by children of that age and location; whether to use clocks with digital or Arabic numerals;

FIGURE 17

Essential Parts of an Item Specification

1. **Objective (or general description)**
   The objective is a clear, precise description of the skill or knowledge to be tested. It should be stated in behavioral terms (what should the students *do* to show they know or can do what is being measured), and it should specify exactly how the skill or knowledge is to be measured.

2. **Sample test item**
   A sample test item is an example of the test items or tasks that are to be used to measure the skill or knowledge described in the objective. It shows exactly what kind of questions, problems, or tasks to present to the student and how the student should respond. The sample test item should include the following:
   - the test directions
   - the question, problem, or task
   - the type of response expected from the student (If the test is multiple choice, the different choices or alternatives should be given. These are called response options.)

3. **Description of how the problem, question, or task should be stated (stimulus attributes)**
   This part of the item specification includes statements that tell item writers the kinds of problems, questions, or tasks that should be written and the way they should be worded. The description of the test problems or questions should state clearly the difficulty level of the questions or prompts; the kinds of words, items, or content that *can be included*; the kinds of words, items, or content that *cannot be included*; the kinds of drawings to use; and other limitations that may be necessary.

4. **Description of how the student should respond (response attributes)**
   This part of the specification lists statements that describe what the student should do or write as his or her response. If the test is multiple choice, the statement specifies the allowable content and the format and difficulty level of the right and wrong answers. If a constructed response is required (if the student is required to write his or her own answer) the description clearly states the criteria or standards for judging correct or incorrect responses. (See Appendix D for samples of scoring criteria.)

whether there should be lines on the clock to indicate one- or five-minute intervals; or whether all numbers should be included or only those at three- or six-hour intervals. (Additional examples of specifications are in Appendix E.)

Who Should Be Involved in Writing Specifications?

It is ideal if several different groups are involved in writing specifications. Measurement specialists who have received training

FIGURE 18

Sample Test Item Specification for Grades 4 to 6 Physical Health: Nutritional Deficiencies

Objective
When presented with a description of an individual with a particular nutrient deficiency disorder or symptom, students will select from a set of options the name of a food that would help alleviate the condition.

Sample test item
    Directions: The person in each description is lacking some nutrient. Find a food that would help solve the problem. Mark the letter of your answer on your answer sheet.

    Obi has aching joints and bleeding gums. His skin bruises very easily. What food should Obi eat?
        a. liver
        b. cassava
        c. mango
        d. yogurt

Description of how the problem or question should be stated
1. Each item will describe, in one to two sentences, a person with the symptoms of a particular nutrient deficiency disorder. Following the description will be the question "What food should (name of person) eat?"
2. Test items will describe deficiency disorders or symptoms arising from a lack of each of the following nutrients: carbohydrates, fats, proteins, calcium, phosphorus, iron, vitamins A, B1 (thiamine), B2 (riboflavin), niacin, C, or D.
3. Each item will describe the symptoms of only one deficiency disorder associated with a given nutrient. For example, a lack of vitamin D can cause rickets and poor development of teeth and bones, but only one of these disorders should be described in a particular item. However, other deficiency disorders of the same nutrient may be described in separate items.
4. Deficiency disorders involving a specific disease will be described rather than named. For example, in the sample item the person has the symptoms of particular disease, but the name of the particular disease is not used.
5. The test will be written at no higher than a grade 4 reading level.

Description of how the student should respond
1. Students will respond by selecting the name of a food that is a good source of the nutrient that would help alleviate the problem described in the stimulus passage.
2. The response set for each item will consist of the correct response and three distracters (wrong answers). Each alternative will name a specific food rather than a category of food type, such as spinach instead of leafy green vegetable or grapefruit instead of citrus fruit.

(continued)

FIGURE 18 *(continued)*

3. Distracters will be selected randomly from the names of foods that do not contain the lacking nutrient. Care must be exercised in choosing distracters for items that describe disorders that might be caused by a lack of different nutrients. For example, retarded growth may be caused by a lack of fats, calcium, phosphorus, or Vitamin B1 (thiamine). The correct response may be chosen randomly from any one of these categories, but food containing good sources of the other nutrients may not be used as distracters.

[*Note: This specification easily could be modified to be culturally and geographically appropriate by changing the names used and foods eaten.*]

From material developed by IOX Assessment Associates, Los Angeles, CA. Adapted by permission.

in criterion-referenced testing should lead the process, but they should be accompanied by subject-matter specialists and classroom teachers. Curriculum developers should be involved because they are most familiar with the curriculum content and with the intention of each topic or theme in the curriculum. Teacher trainers who are knowledgeable about the latest research on teaching and learning in the test subject would also be useful. The individuals involved in writing specifications do not need to be part of the full-time staff of the testing unit; they can meet for periods of time to be trained and to work for several weeks to complete a task. It is possible to have one group write the specifications, another write test items using the specifications, and a third review the items to ensure that they match the specifications and do not contain unintended measurement errors. The items and specifications also need to be reviewed again after they are pilot tested.

There will be some tension between the need to involve teachers and other educators in the test development process and the need to maintain test security. One strategy is to involve teachers in only a small portion of the test development process; another is to develop a large pool of items or tasks for each skill to be tested.

Testing specialists who are trained only in traditional measurement and have not studied criterion-referenced measurement strategies may not be appropriate to include in the specification writing process because traditional measurement techniques are based on different assumptions and strategies than those needed for criterion-referenced testing. Those trained in traditional measurement should receive training in criterion-referenced testing before beginning the test development process.

Specifications are intellectually demanding to write. The best individuals for this task are those who excel in and enjoy analytical

FIGURE 19

Sample Test Item Specifications for Grade 1 Mathematics: Recognizing Shape, Size, and Color

Objective

Given an assortment of objects (such as geometrical shapes), students will sort them according to shape, size, color, or combination of any of the attributes.

Sample test item

Directions: The test will be individually administered. The time required is two minutes per student. The teacher says, "There is a collection of shapes in the box. You must do what I tell you to do and, when you have finished, raise your hand. I will look at what you have done and tell you what to do next. Look in the box and find the objects that are red. [Pause, check the student's answer.] Put the objects back in the box. Now, look in the box and find the objects that are small. [Continue asking the student to find objects with various attributes.]

Stimuli

1. Objects will include rectangles, triangles, and circles of different colors (red, blue, yellow, green) and sizes (big, small, thick, thin).
2. Each item will ask students to select objects on the basis of color, size, and/or shape.

Note: A maximum of two attributes can be used in any one question: for example, small rectangles.

Student responses

The student will select the objects specified by the teacher and place them in the box when directed by the teacher.

Scoring: Beside each criterion, judge the student's answer and then check "yes" if correct or "no" if incorrect. (The scoring key will need to be revised to handle questions with two attributes.)

Criterion	Rating	
	Yes	No
a. Selected objects of the same color.		
b. Selected objects of the same size.		
c. Selected objects of the same shape.		
d. Selected objects of the same color/size combination.		
e. Selected objects of the same color/shape combination.		
f. Selected objects of the same size/shape combination.		

[*Note: Terms and format used in this specification are somewhat different from the others. However, it does provide the information needed to prepare a collection of similar items.*]

From *National Curriculum Centre/Continuous Assessment Unit, EPMT Project,* developed by the Swaziland Ministry of Education, 1992, Mbabane. Adapted by permission.

FIGURE 20

Sample Test Item Specifications for Grade 2 Mathematics: Telling Time

Objective
Given four clock faces with Arabic numerals 1 through 12 indicated at the 5-minute interval markers, students will write the correct time to the half-hour or hour.

Sample test item
Directions: What time does it show on the clocks? Write the correct time under the drawings of the clocks in this form: 7:00.

Description of how the problem or question should be stated
1. Each clock face will be a 6 centimeter-diameter circle.
2. Clock faces will be placed 3 centimeters apart in two horizontal rows.
3. Arabic numerals 1–12 will be placed inside the circle next to the correct 5-minute internal marker.
4. One-minute intervals will not be displayed.
5. The Arabic numerals will be 1/2 centimeters in height.
6. The hour hand on the clocks will be 2 centimeters long. The minute hand will be 3 centimeters long.
7. Test items will not be enclosed by lines.
8. Lines 2 centimeters in length will be centered 2 centimeters under each clock face.
9. No clock face will show 12 noon or midnight.
10. No hour or half-hour time will be duplicated.
11. Two clock faces will show hour times, and the other two will show half-hour times.

Description of how the student should respond
1. The student should write the correct times and include a colon mark between the hour and minute numerals on the line under the clock face.
2. All answers should be given in the same form as the sample item. Other responses such as "seven o'clock" will not be accepted.

From material developed by IOX Assessment Associates, Los Angeles, CA. Adapted by permission.

thinking. It is essential that those who are asked to write specifications be given adequate time and training to do a thoughtful and thorough job. It is important that the specifications are written correctly the first time because they will influence all subsequent test items that are written based on the specifications. However, revisions may be needed based on information gathered from pilot tests of the exams.

As mentioned earlier, the process of writing specifications engages those involved in a detailed analysis of the subject matter to be tested and of how students learn. For these reasons, specification writing is a useful way to enhance teachers' understanding of the curriculum content. Involving all teachers in writing specifications and tests should be considered as an option if a continuous assessment system is being developed. Training teachers in both test development and remediation strategies is a powerful combination. Test development and use also should be a part of preservice teacher training programs.

Writing Specifications May Reveal Weaknesses in the Curriculum and Textbooks

Because the process of writing specifications involves a very close analysis of the curriculum and textbooks to ensure that the tests have curricular and instructional validity, it often reveals flaws in these materials. Here is the dilemma that may arise. A group is charged with the responsibility of writing a test of grade 6 science. As they begin to study the science textbook used by grade 6 students, they notice that the concepts are not explained clearly. They realize that it is unlikely that teachers can accommodate for poor explanations in the texts because many teachers do not have an adequate understanding of the science concepts due to lack of training. The test developers in this situation must choose either to write a test that has curricular and instructional validity but reinforces poor instruction or to develop a test that is consistent with principles of good teaching and learning but may not be consistent with the textbook or curriculum.

One country has decided to solve this dilemma by providing teachers with sets of remedial instructional materials for lessons in the text that are inadequate. Another approach is to revise the textbooks. Textbooks probably are the most influential element in children's learning, particularly in developing countries where teachers' limited subject-matter knowledge often prevents them from being able to compensate for deficiencies in the text. A poorly written text can cause both teachers and students to believe that they are inadequate because they are not able to understand what they are expected to teach or learn. Although there is a growing body of research on how textbooks can be written to enhance understanding and learning, it has not yet influenced textbook development in some countries.

Using Specifications to Communicate with Teachers and Other Educators

A key to influencing better teaching and learning through testing is to communicate to teachers and other educators what quality

A key to influencing better teaching and learning through testing is to communicate to teachers and other educators what constitutes better teaching and learning. © Aga Khan Foundation/Jean-Luc Ray. Used by permission.

teaching and learning is and to use practice tests as a model of quality teaching and learning. There are two times when communication with teachers is most potent: the first is before the tests are given, to signal what will be tested and how, as mentioned earlier; the second is after the tests have been given and the results have been analyzed. Before the tests are given, abbreviated forms of item specifications or practice tasks can be formatted into newsletters or booklets to indicate to teachers what will be on the test. After the test has been administered, test results can be analyzed and reported at various levels

(such as the school or district level), along with suggestions for improvements in areas of greatest weakness. Figure 21 shows an example of how specifications can be used to communicate with teachers before tests are given (see also Appendix F).

A Summary

Item specifications are detailed and precise descriptions of what will be measured, how it will be measured, and the allowable content. They are important to develop for the following reasons.

FIGURE 21

Example of How to Communicate with Teachers About the Purpose of a Writing Assessment

The purposes of this assessment are to provide information to participating schools and districts about the current status of students' writing and to suggest a process that can be used to begin monitoring writing skill development over time. This assessment was designed to influence instruction rather than merely to reflect it. Other purposes of this assessment include the following:

- Encourage more and different types of writing in classrooms.
- Provide information to help teachers strengthen their writing programs.
- Provide information that will reinforce the value of writing.
- Stimulate writing across the curriculum.
- Provide staff development in writing instruction and holistic evaluation.
- Monitor progress toward communication outcomes and writing achievement in schools.
- Measure growth in writing within a school district.
- Provide a measure of the quality of writing within a school district.
- Encourage school districts to develop a systematic program for improving the quality of writing.

Sample prompts
The following directions precede each prompt.

Directions: You will have two sessions to plan your paper, prepare a draft, revise, and write your final copy on the topic given below. You have up to 40 minutes to

- think about what you want to say,
- make notes, and
- write a draft of your paper on the composition paper your teacher has provided.

READ THE ENTIRE PROMPT CAREFULLY.

These directions follow each prompt:

After you have completed your rough draft, read it silently. Be sure you are satisfied with what you have written. Close your text booklet to show that you have finished the draft copy.

From the *Writing Assessment Handbook*, produced by the Pennsylvania State Department of Education, Division of Evaluation and Reports, 1992, Harrisburg. Reprinted by permission.

1. They help ensure that tests are measuring what is *intended*.

2. They serve as a guide for item writers so that all items will be written the same way.

3. They allow banks (or collections) of test items to be produced and used across situations and points in time, and they ensure that all the items that measure a particular ability, skill, or knowledge measure it in the same way and at the same level of difficulty each time the test is administered.

4. They can be used to inform teachers and students about what will be tested and how it will be tested.

Chapter 8 describes how reporting test results also can be used to help influence better teaching and learning and can provide policymakers with useful information for making better policy decisions.

Notes

[1] A statistical approach called "item-response theory" is another way to estimate whether items are measuring the same underlying intellectual abilities—referred to as latent traits. However, this approach generally is applicable to only multiple-choice test items.

CHAPTER 8

Reporting and Using Test Results: A Dialogue with Educators

Reporting test results is one of the few opportunities that policymakers have to converse with teachers and the broader education community about the substance of education. However, discussions among educators tend to focus on the peripherals of teaching and learning—funding, scheduling, construction, salaries, resources, and other factors unrelated to teaching. Although these issues are essential to operating an educational system, they are not the core. The core is teaching and learning. A testing system allows policymakers to focus public attention on what children are learning and what it is that facilitates or hinders their learning.

If a testing system is designed and implemented properly, test results can provide policymakers with solid, reliable, and regular evidence of what is and is not working in schools. Policymakers can use this information to make informed, sound, and thoughtful decisions about the education system. Test results reported regularly reveal changes over time, show whether efforts to improve educational quality are working, and show whether corrective measures are needed and where.

To test without reporting the results to relevant audiences is a waste of time, energy, and money. Student performance on examinations can be aggregated and used as assessment data to compare the performance of schools, districts, and regions and to provide a national-level perspective of student achievement. This is a cost-efficient use of test data. Many countries design and administer examinations and simply report whether individual students did or did not pass the test; teachers, schools, and policymakers do not get the results in a way that can help them make improvements. Test results are a source of valuable data that can be used by different groups of educators throughout the system to analyze and guide efforts to improve teaching and learning.

This chapter describes the policymakers' role in ensuring that test results are used by all relevant audiences; provides examples of test reports that have been used to engage educators in a dialogue about teaching and learning; explains how test results can and should be used equitably; discusses the need to supplement test results with targeted research; explains what information should go into reports aimed at various audiences of educators; and shows how data regarding students' attitudes and background can help explain and supplement the results of students' cognitive achievement. This chapter is *not* intended to be a comprehensive explanation of test reporting procedures. It is focused on the importance of having a variety of educators use test results to guide educational improvement and on the use of test results to influence classroom teachers.

Policymaker's Role

A policymaker's role is to ensure that test results are made available in appropriate formats and are used by all relevant audiences. To fulfill this role, the following steps are necessary:

1. Meet with the testing staff to identify the audiences for test reports and how to address each audience. It is best to initiate this discussion before test development begins and to refine plans at various stages of the process.

2. Encourage the testing staff to meet with each audience to identify their information needs.

3. Budget for the preparation, printing, and dissemination of reports of test results.

4. Allocate sufficient and appropriate staff to the testing unit to ensure that reports of results are disseminated on a timely basis. (Appropriate staff are those who understand both testing *and* teaching and learning.)

5. Budget to bring together groups of educators to discuss the results and to prepare plans for improving the various parts of the educational system based on information provided by test results.

6. Meet with the press to report the results in a way that focuses on teaching and learning.

7. Use the results to argue for budget allocations for staff development, curricular or textbook revision, and development of additional instructional and support materials.

8. Meet with teacher educators to urge and discuss improvements in teacher training based on test results.

9. Ensure that test results are reported fairly.

10. Budget and allocate funds to support follow-up research based on test results.

Promoting a Dialogue

Test results should be reported and disseminated to spur discussion and action— not to blame or accuse. The results should be viewed by all relevant groups and individuals as data that are valid and useful for highlighting strengths and weaknesses and as a tool for solving problems.

Kenya's National Examinations Council has done an excellent job of reporting test results in a way that helps teachers solve instructional problems. The Council publishes the *Kenya Certificate of Primary Education (K.C.P.E.) Newsletter*, which contains test results and provides suggestions to help teachers improve instruction based on an analysis of the results. In this way, the Council communicates with and receives feedback from teachers so that it can improve reporting practices over time. This method exemplifies the notion of a dialogue with teachers about the substance of education—teaching and learning. It illustrates the impact that teachers can have on the reporting process when they are given the opportunity to comment and be heard. The *K.C.P.E. Newsletter* shows how Kenya's teachers value this publication and how the Examinations Council uses it to guide teachers in their efforts to improve teaching and learning. The *Newsletter* serves as a communications bridge between the Kenya Ministry of Education and teachers and headmasters in schools. (Additional sample communications with teachers are shown in Appendix F.)

Sharing Responsibility

There are many elements involved in creating and maintaining an effective education system, and reports of test results should be used by each of the various groups that have a role in that system. Following is a partial list of groups that need the results and an explanation of how each group can use them.

- Teachers can use test results to improve their teaching and to help individual students.

- Principals (or headmasters) can use the results to assist individual teachers and to work with teachers as a group to plan how to improve teaching and learning at the school.

- Staff who are responsible for developing curricula and textbooks can use the results to help identify strengths and weaknesses in the instructional materials and in the curriculum.

- Staff who are responsible for test development can use the results to improve the tests and to provide reports of changes in student achievement over time.

- Teacher trainers can use the results to identify strengths and weaknesses in the teacher training program and to make improvements.

- Inspectors and regional education officers can use test results to guide the nature of the technical assistance and the support they give to schools and teachers.

- Policymakers at district, provincial, state, and national levels can use the results to identify strengths and weaknesses in the system or in parts of the system and to guide efforts to improve teaching and learning.

- Parents want information that will enable them to give their children the best chance they can in light of their long-term aspirations.

Each of these groups should consider the implications of the test results for making improvements in their particular area. Policymakers can ask that each group report their interpretations of the results for their area of responsibility and explain how they intend to use the results to guide practice. For example, Ghana's recent national assessment of grade 6 students showed very poor performance in mathematics. These results spurred an analysis of the grade 6 textbook (Capper, 1994, mentioned in Chapter 1), which revealed that 126 topics were to be covered during the year with approximately 1.49 topics covered each day. In addition, it was discovered that there was an average of 1.25 textbook pages devoted to a topic, and many of the topics were laden with unfamiliar and difficult terminology. Clearly this textbook contains too many topics for students to fully comprehend in the time allotted. This is an instance where test results helped point to problems in a part of the system that may be undermining effective teaching and learning.

The improvement efforts of the various role groups will need to be coordinated, so it would be useful if representatives of each group meet to report their plans and discuss the compatibility and coordination of the plans. In the previous example in Ghana, a meeting of curriculum staff, teachers, teacher trainers, and textbook writers could help clarify the extent of the problem and ways to solve it.

It is also important to encourage parents and community members to get involved in working with their school to review the test results and to develop an action plan for making improvements and setting improvement goals from year to year. Numerous studies have shown the benefits of parent involvement in schools.

One education agency has provided schools with a document that guides them through the process of preparing an action plan for making improvements based on their test results (Massachusetts State Department of Education, 1990). This report outlines the steps in developing an action plan and is intended to be used with other reports that describe subject-area test results for each school. The steps recommended in developing an action plan include the following:

1. Identify the strengths and weaknesses of the school's instructional program (based on subject-area reports of test results).

2. Compare the reports of these test results with other results the school may have.

3. Review the written curriculum, textbooks, and other teaching materials to ensure the topic or skill measured on the test is part of the intended curriculum.

4. Have teachers discuss whether they are teaching the skill, how they are teaching it, if they having problems teaching it, if any of the teachers have particularly successful ways of teaching the skill, ways that the staff can make improvements, and strategies that are working.

5. Identify other factors that may affect student performance, such as poor attendance, lack of instructional materials, unclear or insufficient explanations in textbooks, too many interruptions, or teacher absences.

Research and Test Results

Researchers can use test results to guide them in their search for explanations about what is and is not working in the education system. Researchers should be able to analyze objectively and scientifically the inputs, processes, procedures, and outputs of the system in order to clarify a complex enterprise. Each of the groups of educators listed earlier is likely to view the test results differently and may miss some of the subtle clues that may explain why student achievement is low in one area and high in another or why students in one school outperform or underperform students from similar schools. For example, researchers can help distinguish whether the problems students are having with mixed fractions are due to inadequate explanations in the textbooks, teachers' inadequate understanding or pedagogical skills, or the fact that working with mixed fractions is not developmentally appropriate for students of the age being tested.

Using test results, researchers can identify which schools and classrooms to observe to find the subtle factors that may help or hinder student learning. For example, one study (Evans, 1988) found that in order to raise money for the school, teachers were spending class time selling candy. Test results would not reveal this important finding but could direct the researchers to visit the school to find out why the scores were lower than expected. In another school visited by researchers, the distribution of snacks occupied almost an entire class session. Another study (Ahmed et al., 1993) found that up to 45 minutes a day was lost to roll taking in exceptionally large classes. In fact, the researchers found that when nongovernment schools in which classes of 30 students met for only 3 hours per day were compared to government classes with 100 students who met for 5 hours per day, the smaller 3-hour classes had up to 500 more hours per academic year of on-task learning time. Results such as these have profound implications for policy, technical assistance, and training and can be revealed only if the test results are accompanied by an ongoing, systematic study of schooling by trained and experienced researchers.

It is ideal if a team of researchers is associated with the testing unit early in the process. The researchers could be full-time staff or perhaps faculty from a nearby university. Funds should be allocated for ongoing, timely research, and policymakers should work closely with researchers and testing staff to ensure that the studies conducted meet policymakers' information needs.

Tailoring Reports to the Audience

The use of test results for school improvement should be part of an ongoing process in which results are considered as one set of data among many that are used in an overall system of improvement. For test results to be useful to the various groups of educators listed earlier, the reports of the results must be written in a way that is relevant and understandable for each group. This does not mean that each group should receive a different report. However, at least two reports are required: one for teachers, headmasters, inspectors, teacher trainers, and others who work with teachers on a direct basis and the other for policymakers. There also may be a need for a third report aimed at those responsible for the development, selection, and evaluation of curriculum and instructional materials. This type of report shows students' performance by skill level and facilitates analysis of results in comparison with the curriculum and instructional materials to help identify strengths and weaknesses in the documents.

The report for teachers should be highly readable and relevant to teachers' day-to-day tasks and should provide a detailed analysis of the results with a focus on what those results mean for teaching and learning. Reports for policymakers require less detail regarding specific test items and analyses that relate to instruction but should contain more comparisons—across schools and regions, between urban and rural areas, and between genders. Reports for policymakers also should attempt to correlate results with resources (such as the teacher-student ratio and number of textbooks per student).

What Goes into a Report for Teachers?

Teachers need to know how their students perform overall and on various parts of the test. Results should be reported by subject (for example, mathematics), by skill area or topic (fractions), and by subskill (division of mixed fractions). The more detailed and precise the results, the more information a teacher has to either assist individual students or modify instruction during subsequent school terms. However, detailed and tailored reports are costly and require more staff and time to prepare, and limited resources may constrain the amount of analyses and detail that can be provided in reporting. Regardless of the level of detail in the reports, it is important that teachers receive the reports in a timely manner in order to be relevant and useful—ideally within three or four months after the test has been given.

Reports on test results for teachers should provide several types of comparisons:

- how a school compares with itself over time (how it performed this year compared with last year, or how it is performing compared to goals the school has set for itself);

- how a school compares with other schools in the district, region, or province;

- how a school compares with all schools in the nation (or state); and

- how a school compares with other schools that have similar student bodies.

(Issues about and strategies for making fair comparisons are discussed in a later section of this chapter.)

Kenya's *K.C.P.E. Newsletter*, as mentioned, is an example of a highly readable and relevant report of test results. It speaks directly to teachers, is free of statistical jargon, and provides concrete step-by-step suggestions for teaching those topics on which students performed most poorly. This newsletter is comparable to a teachers' guide, but it has the added benefit of being directly tied to evidence of student performance. Figure 22 contains a slightly modified excerpt from the 1980 *Newsletter*, which reports on Kenya's K.C.P.E. science test and interprets the test results.

Figure 23 shows an excerpt from another example of a useful test report on writing achievement that provides descriptions of each type of writing tested, along with comments of teachers who were involved in the marking process. It also shows the percentage of the students that scored at each level on each type of writing. This report helps reinforce the importance of teaching the various types of writing.

A similar report to the one in Figure 23 was prepared for principals, or headmasters, to provide them with suggestions for how to work with teachers to interpret the test results and to encourage them to use the report as part of their efforts to improve their school program. It suggests that the teachers and principal meet to review and discuss the results and to develop a plan for improving writing instruction at their school. The re-

FIGURE 22

Excerpt from Kenya's Report to Teachers

One of the questions in the science section of the test deserves special mention because so many students answered it incorrectly:

62. Saifa goes to the market to buy a fish. She notices that the pointer of the balance is set as shown in Diagram P. When the fish is placed in the pan, the pointer is as shown in Diagram Q. Which one of the following is the most likely weight of the fish?
    a. 500 grams
    b. 600 grams
    c. 700 grams
    d. 800 grams

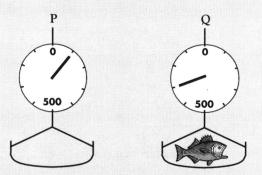

Only 18.5% of rural candidates and 20.1% of Nairobi candidates (excluding those in high-cost and private schools) correctly worked out that the most likely weight of the fish was 600 grams. More than 4% of candidates in both samples chose 700 grams. This, of course, is the reading shown in the second diagram (Q), with the fish in the pan. These candidates ignored the information given in the first diagram (P), which shows that before the fish was placed in the pan the pointer was set to 100 grams. Thus the fish probably weighs 100 grams less than the reading shown in Q. If Saifa made the same mistake as these candidates, she probably paid too much for this fish!

When a customer buys sugar, meat, or fish from a shop, or when a farmer sells his pyrethrum, coffee, or maize, he needs to be able to check that the weighing is done accurately. During geography and science fieldtrips, pupils should become familiar with as many different types of balances and scales as possible. Pupils can observe weighing being carried out in places such as coffee factories, post offices, and tea centres (places where tea farmers sell their green tea leaves) as well as shops and markets.

From the *Kenya Certificate of Primary Education (K.C.P.E.) Newsletter*, produced by the Kenya National Examinations Council, 1980, Nairobi. Used by permission.

FIGURE 23

Excerpt from California's Report of Writing Achievement: 1990

Types of writing tested: Autobiographical Incident and Evaluation
Type of scoring: Coherence

Comments from teacher markers

"Autobiographical incident requires both the 'auto' and the 'incident.' Students who were uncomfortable with the 'I' and those who roamed from incident to situation to phase became accident victims."

"In writing as in autobiography and prose fiction, an incident can be defined, recognized, and written. We must work back and forth between the reading of literature and the writing of autobiographical incident."

"We must not give students a set introduction to use with all autobiographical incidents; formula writing is directly antithetical to all that we strive for in autobiography—the strong sense of self that an effective paper achieves."

Autobiographical Incident

Writers narrate an incident from their personal experience. They orient readers to the incident and they may include dialogue, movement or gestures, names of people or objects, and sensory details. Writers describe their remembered feelings, understandings, or reflections at the time of the incident; and they also may evaluate the incident from their present perspective, implying or stating its significance in their lives.

Essays scored 6 include several of the strategies and use them in an effective, engaging way. Essays scored 1 reflect few if any of the autobiographical strategies. Essays scored 3 or 4 narrate a less well-developed incident, making only limited use of the strategies.

	Autobiographical Incident Rhetorical Effectiveness Scores							
	6	5	4	3	2	1	Off topic	No response
Percentage of students	1	13	25	39	17	6	0	0

(continued)

FIGURE 23 (continued)

Comments from teacher markers

"Evaluation is as natural as breathing."

"I now see that formula evaluations won't 'sneak' by the scoring guide with unmerited success. We must not try to teach to this test by drilling students in formulaic writing."

"There is a major difference between assigning evaluation and teaching evaluation. With the clear descriptions available in the writing handbook, we can easily make evaluation understandable for students; we need to provide them with a range of strategies and give them good models to follow."

"Abolish book reports! Instead, show your students how to go beyond summary-style reports. Teach evaluation—the positive side of discrimination—and help students learn to establish logical and appropriate criteria."

Evaluation

Writers state a judgment of something (movie, book, author, teacher, sports team, or consumer product) and support their judgment with evidence. They may describe the subject being evaluated but should not allow the description to dominate the essay. Mainly, they develop one or more supporting ideas to justify their judgment. Evidence may come from personal experience as well as from the writer's careful analysis and thoughtful understanding of the subject.

Essays scored 6 present a well-supported judgment. Essays scored 1 do not present evidence supporting a judgment. Essays scored 3 or 4 offer only a moderately developed argument supporting a judgment.

	Evaluation Rhetorical Effectiveness Scores							
	6	5	4	3	2	1	Off topic	No response
Percentage of students	2	14	23	28	27	2	3	0

From *Survey of Academic Skills: Writing Achievement, Grade 12, 1989–90* (California Assessment Program), produced by the California State Department of Education, 1990, Sacramento. Adapted by permission.

port also suggests that teachers and the principal meet regularly to share successful strategies and to evaluate their progress and that the school faculty explore ways to teach writing within the various curricular areas.

What Goes into a Report for Policymakers?

Although there are basic data that should be included in all reports of test results for policymakers, additional analyses and reporting could be done if funds and appropriately trained staff are available. Also, staff may need to decide whether to prepare a report that contains limited information but is more likely to be read because it can be read quickly or to prepare a report with an abundance of information that may cause the busy policymaker to procrastinate reading such a lengthy document. It is probably best to begin with a brief report and to add analyses and data that come from direct requests.

The basic information that should be contained in all reports of test results for policymakers is as follows:

- Achievement data by grade, subject, skill area (such as chemistry—structure of matter, periodic classification, or states of matter), gender, school, district, region or province, and nation.

- Achievement data by each of the factors just mentioned over a specified number of years.

- Number of students tested in each of the listed categories; number of students who did *not* sit for the test in each school or classroom.

- Sample test items.

- Scoring criteria and approaches to scoring, particularly for open-ended, essay, and performance tests.

- Analysis and interpretation of results with possible implications for policymakers.

- Explanations of technical approaches used in test development and in analysis of test results.

- Analysis and interpretation of attitudinal, behavioral, or comparison data if collected.

Although there are various ways to represent data (such as with graphs, charts, and tables) that would be helpful to policymakers, one example is shown in Figure 24. This figure offers comparisons of student achievement by school, district, and region and by other factors.

Allocating Accountability Fairly

If students' test results are poor, the blame usually is placed on teachers. An important step in ensuring that test results are reported fairly is to take into account other factors that can influence learning achievement. In addition to effective teaching, there are two major categories of factors that influence student learning, and both should be considered in the reporting and use of test results. The first category is the external factors over which schools and teachers have no control—factors such as parental education, family income, and students' primary language. For example, urban parents are more likely to send girls to school and to send them regularly than are rural parents, and urban chil-

FIGURE 24

Student Achievement Comparing Performance by School, District, and Region and by Sex, Parents' Level of Education, and English-Language Proficiency

School _____
District _____

Subgroup, by Sex, Parent Education, and English Proficiency	School			District			Region	
	No.	Students %	Scaled score	No.	Students %	Scaled score	Students %	Scaled score
All Students	369	100	259	1847	100	269	100	256
Sex								
Male	157	43	237	803	43	253	48	237
Female	206	56	277	983	53	283	49	277
Parent Education								
Advanced degree	30	8	321	169	9	321	13	320
College graduate	73	20	292	358	19	303	20	283
Some college	78	21	269	470	25	273	22	267
Secondary graduate	68	18	245	348	19	258	16	231
Primary graduate	39	11	191	166	9	206	13	196
English Proficiency							82	265
English only	310	84	270	1613	87	276	12	243
plus primary language	26	7	246	105	6	275	5	153
Limited English plus primary language	33	9	161	129	7	169		

From *Survey of Academic Skills: Writing Achievement, Grade 12, 1989–90* (California Assessment Program), produced by the California State Department of Education, 1990, Sacramento. Adapted by permission.

dren are less likely to be absent from school due to family responsibilities such as farming or childcare. The second category refers to those factors that the educational system can influence but over which teachers have little control, such as the curriculum, textbooks, teacher training, policies, support, resources, and facilities.

Comparing schools that have substantial disparities in their resources, situations, and contexts does not provide a fair or realistic picture of what is reasonable to expect of teachers and students. A more equitable approach is to gather data on the factors that are hypothesized to make a difference in students' learning (such as parental education, level of teacher qualification, primary language, urban or rural school location, number of textbooks and access to teacher and curriculum guides, and quality of school libraries), but over which schools have little or no control, and to use this data to place schools in groups for purposes of analyzing and reporting test results. For example, all remote schools that have no electricity or buildings, where most of the parents have not completed primary school, should be compared with other similar schools. Urban schools, where most parents have completed high school or college, that have high-quality facilities and better educated teachers should be compared with other similar schools. The factors that are used for these comparisons should be those over which the education system has little or no control. For example, teacher or student absences should *not* be considered because schools do have control over absences and this would legitimize their not trying to control absences.

Kenya's National Examinations Council has attempted to make more equitable comparisons by separating rural schools from urban schools and by distinguishing those from the high-cost and private schools (see Figure 25).

Criticisms of Comparing Schools Using Test Results

Not all people agree on the practice of evaluating schools based on test results. Opponents of this practice contend that the comparisons often do not take into account differences in the types of students and the social or physical conditions of the schools; school rankings can vary depending on the measure that is used; errors in measurement are seldom taken into account; and schools can manipulate pass rates by improper practices such as not promoting students or not accepting students into the school who they believe will not reflect well on the school. In addition, publicizing comparisons based on test results can lead to transfers of better teachers, low morale in low-achieving schools, parents' moving so their children can go to schools with better scores, and in some cases closings of schools due to declining enrollments (Greaney & Kellaghan, 1995).

Reporting Open-Ended and Performance Test Results

Reporting of student performance on open-ended questions and performance tasks is more complicated than for multiple-choice items. However, as with essay testing, it is important to convey the criteria used to judge student performance. Figure 26 shows a summary of results and a scoring guide for an open-ended mathematics question administered to grade 12 students. The whole mathematics test contained five open-ended questions, and there were different criteria used to judge performance on each question. In addition, teachers were provided with a procedure for developing their own scoring guides for use in their classrooms. The procedure teachers were given follows:

1. Have students work the open-ended problem.

Example of a Test Report Showing Equitable Comparisons of Rural and Urban Schools

Average raw marks in the 1980 English objective paper were as follows, with the 1979 and 1980 figures for comparison:

Average Mark

	1980	1979
Rural schools	43.7%	42.2%
Nairobi schools (excluding high-cost and private schools)	50.1%	51.3%
Performance gap	6.4%	9.1%

In rural schools, the average mark rose by 1.5% between 1979 and 1980, whereas in Nairobi schools, the average dropped by 1.2%. The Nairobi sample excludes government schools that charge fees and also private schools. The Nairobi schools still enjoy an advantage over the rural schools in English, but between 1979 and 1980 the performance gap dropped from 9.1% to only 6.4%.

In the rural schools, boys performed a little better than girls, but the performance gap was lower [in English] than for any other subject.

Subject	1980			1979		
	Boys	Girls	Gap	Boys	Girls	Gap
English	44.9	41.9	3.0	43.6	40.0	3.6
Science	48.3	42.4	5.9	49.9	42.2	7.7

[Note: Similar data were given for each of five subject areas.]

From the *Kenya Certificate of Primary Education (K.C.P.E.) Newsletter*, produced by the Kenya National Examinations Council, 1981, Nairobi. Used by permission.

2. Have faculty colleagues in mathematics do the same problem.

3. Discuss the problem with faculty, and try to sort the students' papers into six groups, with six being the highest rank and one the lowest.

4. Discuss the characteristics of the responses and articulate a scoring guide for an exemplary rating response.

5. Articulate scoring guides for the other categories.

6. Take a second look at the students' papers and, based on the scoring guides, regroup them as needed.

The report of open-ended results in Figure 26 specifies the general expectations of students in solving one of the five problems tested, provides an analysis of the strengths and weaknesses in students' responses, shows sample student responses, describes misconceptions represented by the various responses, and suggests implications based on an analysis of the misconceptions. This is followed by a summary of the results for the problem and general instructional implications.

Although these open-ended mathematics problems were administered to many students, only a sample of responses were scored. If these items were to be used to judge individual students for certification or selection purposes, all responses would need to be scored. However, if the intent is to leverage better teaching and learning, only a sample of responses would need to be scored; to increase the likelihood that teachers will emphasize teaching open-ended problems, the testing agency could convey that these types of items will be on the test but not specify which will be used for selection or certification or which will be used to assess performance at the system or subsystem level.

Using Attitude and Background Data to Help Explain Test Results

Some school systems collect attitudinal and background data on students when tests are administered to identify some of the factors that may influence student learning. For example, the California State Department of Education (1989b) found that students in grade 4 who read "almost every day" scored more than 150 points higher on a state assessment than did students who "never or hardly ever" read for pleasure. Another interesting finding was that students in grades 8 and 12 who spent at least an hour a day on homework scored approximately 100 to 150 points higher on the test than those who spent less time. Further, students who watched more than three hours a day of television scored significantly lower than those students who watched less; students who talk about school with someone at home had higher test scores; and students who had opportunities to apply what they learned in a work setting had slightly higher scores than students who did not work, but as the number of hours of work increased, the test scores declined. Students also reported that they did not consider what they were learning in science, social studies, and mathematics very useful, and more than 40 percent of both grade 8 and 12 students see their math and science courses as "mainly memorizing."

This valuable data was collected at the time of the examination and can be useful in many ways. For example, school officials may ask the news media to report these particular findings as a way to convey the role of parents in nurturing their children's learning by turning off the television or encouraging their children to read. This is another opportunity to share the responsibility for educating children. The California report of students' attitudes and views relating to test performance documents students' perceptions regarding the type of instruction that is practical in classrooms and provides evidence for use in encouraging teachers to use strategies that promote understanding rather than memorization.

Using Results for Test Improvement

Test results also should be used to help determine the validity and reliability of tests. As mentioned, validity depends in part on

FIGURE 26

Excerpt from Report of Student Performance on an Open-Ended Mathematics Problem

Problem

James knows that half the students from his school are accepted at the public university nearby. Also, half are accepted at the local private college. James thinks that this adds up to 100, so he surely will be accepted at one or the other institution. Explain why James may be wrong. If possible, use a diagram in your explanation.

General Expectations

An important aspect of mathematical power is the need to use logic and diagrams to make sense of a situation and to communicate this reasoning. Diagrams are an effective analytical and communications tool. The problem assesses the ability to detect erroneous reasoning and requires a clear and mathematically correct explanation of the faulty reasoning. Specifically, the problem demands a recognition that acceptances from the different institutions are not mutually exclusive. The students' responses should focus on the faulty reasoning involving James's assumption of nonoverlapping sets. A variety of diagrams or explanations could be used to help clarify the situation; no particular one was preferred.

Strengths and Weaknesses in Students' Responses

Of the students who succeeded in understanding and solving this problem, all were able to make a statement to the effect that some students may be accepted at both schools.

This type of response was judged to be adequate in showing a grasp of the problem, but good responses included more complete explanations with examples and/or counterexamples and diagrams that clarified the reasoning. In fact, the variety of diagramming techniques was very exciting and included Venn diagrams, picture diagrams, keyed lists, comic strips, and pie graphs or charts. The diagrams used by those who were successful in solving this problem indicate that at least some students have had opportunities to create and analyze such models in their mathematics instruction. The following examples illustrate good responses from students.

Example 1

Example 2

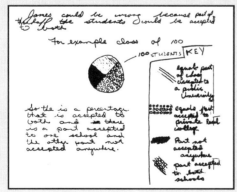 

(continued)

FIGURE 26 *(continued)*

Students whose responses were inadequate digressed from the problem, focusing on extraneous factors such as grades or graduation requirements. Others simply were unable to make sense of the problem and gave inappropriate answers or made misleading assumptions. The committee members identified some of the common misconceptions and made the suggestions to assist in classroom instruction, as follows.

Misconception

Students questioned the hypotheses of the problem, made inappropriate assumptions, or did not correct James's reasoning.

Teaching Implications

Students should be asked to distinguish among the given conditions of a situation, hidden assumptions, and unjustified assumptions. Students should articulate their reasoning in evaluating their own and their peers' reasoning. In addition to having students do formal proofs using theorems, teachers should provide time for frequent group discussion, writing, and drawing of diagrams.

Misconception

Students often resorted to meaningless manipulation of symbols when confronted with a new problem situation. For example, one student unsuccessfully attempted to produce an equation to represent the situation.

Teaching Implications

The emphasis in the classroom should be on discussing and developing appropriate strategies rather than on simply finding an answer.

Misconception

Students were unable to provide an appropriate diagram to enhance their explanations.

Teaching Implications

Students need more opportunities to read, interpret, and create charts, tables, diagrams, and graphs. They should be able to abstract mathematical information from a situation and develop a model that represents the information.

Misconception

Students used an invalid assumption that the number of students was odd in attempting to prove that James's inference was incorrect.

Teaching Implications

Students should be taught the use of tools such as Venn diagrams in order to identify false inferences in situations involving logic.

(continued)

Summary of Results and Instructional Implications

Of the approximately 500 papers scored, only 20% of the responses showed that students were able to explain, with or without the help of diagrams, that an overlap can exist between the groups admitted to the college and the university. Approximately 25% of the students in the sample digressed from the point of the problem. Another 40% were unable to interpret the situation sensibly and gave inappropriate answers.

In summary, the sample of responses to this problem showed a great need for an increase in experiences for all secondary students with diagrams and graphs, nonroutine problems, and recognition and interpretation of faulty reasoning.

Although students and teachers should become accustomed to accepting and encouraging a variety of responses, we recommend that teachers help students focus on what the problem asks for. Students should identify important information and avoid using added considerations that are not relevant to solving the problem.

From A *Question of Thinking: A First Look at Students' Performance on Open-Ended Questions in Mathematics* (California Assessment Program), produced by the California State Department of Education, 1989, Sacramento. Adapted by permission.

how the test results are used, so the validity of a test may vary from time to time or from one use to another. For example, if the results are to be used to certify students at the end of primary school, and the results are substantially different from students' grades or from other relevant test scores, this would indicate that the test may not be entirely valid—it may not accurately measure the curriculum or instruction. Or it may mean that students' grades are not valid indicators of students' achievement in learning.

Another possibility for the discrepancy in test results could be that the test may match the curriculum, but there may be certain skills or important concepts that are not explained adequately in the teacher's guide or textbook. Teachers may not have sufficient understanding of the skills, or concepts simply are not taught. In this situation, the test would be valid with regard to the curriculum but not to instruction. This does not mean that the test should be discarded; an option would be to gather more information from teachers about why they are not teaching those particular skills and concepts and decide how to facilitate their instruction.

When textbooks are prepared, quite often the hopes and expectations about what can be covered are substantially greater than the reality. Overcrowded classrooms, limited resources and training, and frequent absences can contribute to less instructional time than was intended by textbook writers. In this case, the curriculum, textbook, and test all may need revision.

Another problem may be that there are unrealistic assumptions about what is appropriate for students to learn at various developmental levels. In this instance, topics that should be covered at higher grade levels are included in texts for younger students, resulting in poor test performance. Test developers may need to work with teachers, developmental psychologists, curriculum specialists, and textbook writers to review potential causes and solutions in this situation.

Each time the test is administered, the results also should be used to determine if the test is reliable. As mentioned, one of the reasons to prepare item specifications is to produce homogeneous items for each subtest. For example, if mastery of a particular skill is to be demonstrated by performance on six test items, it is important that all six items measure the skill consistently. If two items differ in content or format from the other four, incorrect conclusions might be drawn about students who succeeded on different combinations of items. If the results show that some items written to a specification are very easy for students and others are very difficult, the items are not homogeneous and will need to be changed. It is likely that the specifications also will need to be revised to ensure that items written to the specification are more homogeneous.

A Final Word

Tests are an essential tool to monitor and evaluate student achievement, and test results should be used by educators at all levels for guiding school improvement efforts. Reports of results must be prepared with the particular audience in mind. They should be preceded by detailed analyses of why particular results were obtained and followed by research studies to further understand factors that help or hinder student learning.

CHAPTER 9

A Checklist for Achieving a Better Testing System and Avoiding Difficulties

Initiating changes to improve a testing system can be a daunting task. This chapter presents several suggestions for avoiding potential difficulties with introducing changes in a testing system.

Avoid Teacher Resistance by Making Fewer Initial Changes

Probably the greatest threat to making changes toward an improved testing system is teacher resistance. Many people feel uncomfortable, awkward, and slightly embarrassed when trying to learn something new. New forms of assessment may require that teachers learn new skills and spend additional time and energy in the classroom.

Teacher resistance was found to be a problem in the United Kingdom when a new national curriculum and assessment system was implemented. Reports of the impact of the pilot activity offer suggestions about practices that might be wise to avoid (Torrance, 1993). The national assessment began with large and complex authentic tasks for use with children at age seven. The multidimensional task that was pilot tested was designed to require a minimum of three weeks to complete but allowed a full term. Some reports from teachers indicated that this was too large an assess-

ment with which to begin. Most teachers spread the tasks over about five weeks and often did not finish them. The overall assessment included several subtasks such as rolling toy cars down slopes of different gradients to encourage students to investigate how far they traveled and why, using dice in a simple game to test computational skills, and drawing and labeling a poster to illustrate how and why things grow.

Several teachers reported that they felt overwhelmed by the assessment process. They worked two to three extra hours every evening and six hours each weekend on marking, record keeping, gathering resources, and planning the next day's work. Teachers also reported that it was difficult to balance management of the whole class while focusing on individual students and small groups to gather assessment data. In addition, because the tasks had been designed centrally, teachers were unfamiliar with them and constantly had to refer to the tasks as they were teaching. They felt deskilled and overly dependent on the guidance materials that had been delivered to them, as the following quotes (Torrance, 1993, pp. 86, 88) demonstrate:

"I felt threatened by presenting materials I had not devised and restricted to certain actions/words. I had to look everything up before I spoke....I needed to be rigidly organized to feel secure when presenting these."

"This problem was exacerbated by the high stakes atmosphere surrounding the pilot, which emphasized issues of accountability rather than what might be gained from a less pressurized exploration of new approaches to assessment."

Conversely, teachers also viewed the new assessment activities as more exciting and challenging for the children than the curriculum typically provided in schools. Although the teachers expressed discomfort, the process ultimately resulted in better learning for their students.

Gipps (1990) suggests how introducing the new assessment system in the United Kingdom might have been handled differently:

> It is of course unfortunate to say the least that this is to happen on the backs of practicing teachers and children. How much better it would have been to have had an experimental development project which tested out the Task Group on Assessment and Testing model and not to have implemented it nationally until we knew it would work. But that takes time and such are the political realities that this was not possible. (p. 279)

Because teachers in developing countries are unlikely to have the training, education, or resources available to UK teachers, they may be more overwhelmed with new assessments. Gipps (1990) believes that a better approach to implementing changes would be to start small. Instead of beginning with an assessment that incorporates several complex tasks, an assessment that focuses on just one task and one subject area may be more well received by teachers because they will have time to become comfortable with the changes. Teachers need time and space to explore and learn. They need to feel free to debate and disagree and to believe that they can influence assessment practices. They need to feel that they can be part of an overall effort to help improve teaching and learning in schools and that others are not dictating what happens in the classroom.

Other strategies that may reduce teachers' resistance include the following:

- Involve teachers in the design of the assessment.

- Show teachers a sample of the assessment measures and allow them time to try them without the threat of consequences.

- Get feedback from teachers.

- Make revisions based on teacher feedback.

- Let teachers know their concerns have been heard and responded to.

- Provide training in how to use the new assessments and how to teach in ways that are consistent with the assessment measures.

- Provide training in curricular areas that may be affected by the new assessments or by changes in the curriculum or instructional materials.

- Dispatch trained observers to document teachers' use of the assessments at the pilot stage. Make sure that these observers do not evaluate or convey judgments to teachers but stress that they are only there to get feedback for making improvements in the assessments and the system.

- Make a team of coaches available—possibly inspectors, head teachers, or teacher trainers—who can help teachers learn new ways of teaching and assessing.

- Think of implementing changes in a testing system as a long-term process—not a quick fix.

Discourage Low Expectations

Teachers of low-achieving students may feel that open-ended or performance tasks that focus on thinking and problem-solving skills are inappropriate for their students. Badger (1995) found that U.S. teachers of students in low-achieving schools did not think their students could answer open-ended or performance-type tasks. They believed that the tasks required more independent thinking than their students could handle: "My students aren't used to it. We need to make the question-answer better. Lead the children to draw specific conclusions by specific questioning" (pp. 6–7).

However, contrary to the teachers' expectations, Badger (1995) found that overall low-achieving students performed better on the open-ended questions than on multiple-choice questions. Students from the more advantaged schools performed about the same or slightly worse on the open-ended questions, although they performed significantly better than the disadvantaged students overall.

The implication of this study is that because teachers in low-achieving schools do not expect their students to be able to think

and solve problems, they tend not to include these skills in their instruction. However, there is considerable evidence that all students can think at higher cognitive levels and can enjoy solving problems—even students who may not have mastered the basic skills. It should be made clear that *all* teachers are expected to engage *all* students in active learning that promotes thinking and problem solving. Not all students may be able to think at the same cognitive level or solve problems using the same level of content, but all can engage in these important skills.

Check the Consequences of Changes in Testing Programs or Policies

Testing systems that use performance-based, authentic assessments usually are designed to enhance teaching and learning. Therefore, for a test to be valid for this purpose, it must accomplish its goal of enhancing teaching and learning. This means that studies of the validity of the assessment consequences must be conducted, which require a clear statement about what the tests are intended to accomplish. For example, if the tests are expected to have an impact on what and how teachers teach, the statement should describe exactly what teachers are expected to do and how they are expected to do it. The statement should specify if the tests lead teachers to change the nature of the assignments they give students or change the way they allocate time in the classroom. If so, what kinds of reallocations are desired? Classroom observations of a sample of schools will be needed to determine if the tests have the intended effects or have undesired outcomes.

Authentic assessments also are expected to motivate students to work harder in school and enjoy learning. Do they accomplish this? Do all students like school better? Which students are affected negatively? positively? Are dropout rates higher? Is attendance lower? Do students perform better at the next level? Do the assessments have an adverse impact on minority ethnic or language groups, rural students, low-income students, or girls?

Anticipate Parental Resistance

Parents typically are very concerned that their children do well on examinations. Even though they may feel that the current examinations are unfair, or they may have other complaints about them, parents are at least familiar with the examinations. They also may be resistant to any changes in the examinations.

To anticipate, and perhaps avoid, parental resistance to changes in tests, it may be useful to meet with groups of parents to explain the proposed changes and the rationale behind the changes, to ask parents about their concerns, and to try engage them as partners in the reforms.

Understand Inequities That Influence Examination Performance

There are various factors that may cause students to perform poorly on examinations, and not all the factors are attributable to students' deficiencies. A recent World Bank publication by Greaney and Kellaghan (1995) describes several sources of inequities that may influence students' performance on examinations, many of which are due to the limited and perhaps inequitably distributed economic resources for education. Disparities in resources can influence substantially the quality of instruction that is made available to students. Several of the factors that contribute to inequity in teaching and learning and in examination performance are described following.

Inequitable Use of Examinations for Accountability Purposes

Because schools often are evaluated on the basis of their students' examination scores, exams may contribute to undesirable practices. There is evidence that in order to gain a positive reputation, some schools either do not admit students who are not likely to succeed on examinations, do not promote certain students, discourage them from taking the examinations, or encourage them to leave school at an early age (Oloo, 1990). Wen (1993) reported that in China as many as 20 percent of students are held back in the second year of middle school in order to raise the level of school performance on the college matriculation examination.

Using examination results to compare schools may fail to take into account the many variables that can influence examination scores but are beyond the school's ability to influence. For example, rural schools often employ teachers who are not as well trained as those in urban areas, and these schools often have fewer resources. The educational and economic background of parents also may be lower in rural areas than in urban areas.

If statistical adjustments were made for these factors, schools might be ranked very differently. Chapter 8 contains strategies for considering some of these factors when reporting test results.

Inequitable Test Items

Bias. Tests sometimes can have differential effects on various groups of students, such as girls and boys, students in urban and rural areas, language groups, or socioeconomic groups. The differential effect may be due to biases in test items.

How can someone determine when a test item is biased? There is not a single definition of bias, but the following definition should apply to test items, or questions, as used in certification or selection examinations or in national assessment measures:

> An item of a test is said to be biased for members of a particular group if, on that item, the members of the group obtain an average score that differs from the average score of other groups by more or less than expected from performance on other items on the same test. (Cleary & Hilton, 1968, p. 61)

In other words, a biased test item is one that contains a characteristic that causes one group to respond differently to that item than another group. Somerset (1993) identified the following question that may be biased against rural students and even poor urban students: "Today we have machines for everything...for washing clothes and washing dishes...and mechanical apparatus for cooking and cleaning. Can you be sure of the changes machines will bring in the lives of future generations? Give reasons."

Fairness. One definition of bias is any test that results in a systematic difference in scores among groups. However, with this definition, all tests would be biased because one group will always score systematically lower than another group. Consider, for example, a situation in which an examining board has identified and revised or deleted biased items from its selection examination, but students from a poor rural area still score systematically lower than do students from resource-rich urban schools. This difference in scores may not be the result of biased test items but rather of unfairness, of the effect of a history of differential treatment of and opportunities for persons from the poor rural areas (California State Department of Education, 1979b).

This systematic difference in scores among groups may indicate that, for various reasons, the educational system has not been successful in meeting the academic needs of some segments of the student population. To claim that the problem lies with the tests is to imply that educationally disadvantaged students are proficient in the basic skills, and the tests simply are not reflecting their proficiency.

Bias refers to how a test is constructed, and fairness refers to how a test is used. Although values and judgments influence estimates of fairness, decisions regarding the fair use of a test must be made irrespective of the presence or absence of bias. Here is an example of unfair uses of a test. A test of computation skills is used to determine which students will be required to take a remedial math class. The test contains items designed to measure consumer math skills.

Students in grades 6 and 7 perform poorly on the test because consumer math is not taught until grade 8; it is also not taught in the remedial course. Unless these consumer math items are deleted from the test or unless students are taught consumer math before taking the test, using the test to determine who is required to take a remedial math course would be considered an unfair use of the test.

It is also possible that some students possess the computation skills required to pass the test but fail because they are unable to read the questions in the language in which it is given. In this event, requiring a remedial math course would be both inappropriate and unfair to the students. An approach to overcoming such a problem is to remove the need for reading skills by either reading the questions to the students or designing the test so that no reading is required to understand the questions.

If a disproportionate number of a particular group of students performs poorly on the examination, then the exam may be carrying forward the effects of prior discrimination, either deliberate or unintended through deficient educational resources. These students may be denied access to many opportunities because of unequal treatment in the past. The remedy is not to make corrections in the examination, but rather to correct the disproportionate allocation of resources.

How to identify biased test items. The identification of biased test items should be conducted in two phases: (1) before administering the field test, the actual test items should be reviewed by a committee; and (2) after administering the field test, results should be reviewed. Larger field-test samples will yield more reliable estimates of the potential for bias.

Phase 1: Reviewing test items before the field test. This procedure involves looking carefully at each test item and determining whether the content of the item is either inappropriate or biased for the groups of students whose skills are being assessed. If an item looks like it may be especially more difficult for one group than another, it is probably biased and should be eliminated.

Reviews of test items for bias should be conducted by a committee composed of members who are sensitive to the concerns of the groups they represent. Representatives of the following might be included:

- all ethnic and language groups in the country
- rural and urban residents
- classroom teachers from various subject areas who represent various geographic, ethnic, and linguistic groups
- gender-sensitive females and males
- economically disadvantaged groups
- a testing specialist

Items also should be reviewed for gender balance. Greaney and Kellaghan (1995) found that differences in examination performance between boys and girls appear to vary substantially among countries. In some countries boys consistently outperform girls (such as in Sudan, Zimbabwe, Tanzania, Malawi, and Kenya), but girls outperform boys in others (in Mauritius and the Caribbean countries). Some test items may not necessarily be biased against one or the other gender, but there is considerable evidence that girls are not equally or fairly represented in tests or textbooks. In a review of part of Ghana's grade 6 national assessment test of English (Capper, 1994), males were referred to 39 times, compared to only 12 times for females. Of the 39 references for males, 19 were positive, 17 were neutral, and only 3 were negative. For female references, only 1 of the 12 was positive, and 6 were negative. Following is an example of a reading passage in which a girl is negatively portrayed:

> Last Sunday, Aku sat all day watching television. She didn't do her homework because she thought she could do it on Monday morning. But she failed to complete the work before going to school. When the teacher asked for her work, she began to cry. The teacher asked her to stop crying and gave her time to finish the work during the morning break.

In this passage, not only is the girl depicted as lazy, "Aku sat all day watching television," but when confronted with the consequences of her laziness, she retreats to "typical" girl behavior—she cries. In contrast, boys referred to in other passages in the test are in professional positions—a king, tailor, lawyer, doctor, or minister. Or they are in positions of power ("John's father has bought a new car") or action ("Odame has scored a goal"). When females are referred to, they often perform poorly ("She doesn't play ampe well, does she?") or are victims of bad luck ("Mame Badu, the cloth seller, has a swollen foot").

Even after some U.S. testing companies became sensitized to possibilities of gender and ethnic bias in tests, a 1984 analysis of tests found twice as many references to men as to women and more pictures of and references to boys than girls. Even male animals were listed almost twice as often as female animals (Selkow, 1984). In another study analyzing the SAT, there were 42 references to men and only 3 to women in the reading comprehension passages used in the four 1984–1985 examinations. Moreover, of the 42 men, 34 were famous and their work was cited; only 1 of the women cited was famous and her work was criticized (*Fairness in Standardized Testing*, 1987).

It should be noted that there is no solid evidence that disparities in gender representation result in differences in test scores.

Phase 2: Identifying biased items using field-test results. Several statistical approaches have been developed for using field-test results to examine the interaction between test items and groups. However, when the approaches were compared with one another, the results revealed that except for a very few cases each approach identified different items on the same test as being biased. (This may be due to the variations in definitions and assumptions underlying the approaches.) In addition, most of these approaches are fairly complex and time consuming.

The purpose of analyzing field-test results is not to determine whether there is a difference between the overall scores of various groups, but rather to identify test items that are more difficult for one group than would be expected based on the group's overall performance and to provide information to make decisions on how to revise the measure accordingly. The steps in a simplified approach to identifying biased test items are as follows:

1. Administer each of the subtests that make up the examination. When con-

ducting the field test, provide teachers and older students with forms on which to indicate their perceptions of any test item or test directions that are unclear. (See Figure 27 for a sample form.) The test administrator should tell students that the test is being given as a field test and that the results will be used only to refine the test or to revise the instructional program, not to give grades, to award or deny certificates, or to make school selections.

2. Sort subtest results by the ethnic, gender, language, geographic, and socioeconomic status groups that are of concern.

3. For each subtest within a content area, calculate the percent correct value of each item for each group. A percent correct value is determined by dividing the number of correct responses to an item by the total number of students who responded to the item, as shown:

$$\text{percent correct value} = \frac{\text{number of correct responses to item}}{\text{number of students who responded to the item}}$$

(Percent correct values range from 0.1 to 1.0. Lower numbers indicate that the item is more difficult; higher numbers indicate easier items.)

4. For each subtest, list the percent correct value for each item by group, as indicated in Table 2.

5. Draw a vertical axis for each group and mark it by intervals that coincide with the percent correct value scores (see Table 3). Place an "x" next to the appropriate percent correct value on this vertical axis for each item. Continue this process for the remaining items and groups. The scores for the subtests should not be combined; separate graphs should be plotted for each subtest.

After identifying which items may be more difficult for some groups, it is important to review all response alternatives (the possible answers given in multiple-choice tests), identify the alternative most frequently chosen by each group, and examine the item stem (the part of the test item that provides the question or statement to which examinees are to respond) and directions for clarity. It also may be useful to ask several students who missed the item to explain why they responded as they did. It may be necessary to discard the item in favor of an improved item.

Gender bias in selection examinations. There is evidence that standardized selection examinations do not fairly represent girls' ability. Although the SAT is designed to predict college success defined by first-year grades, the test consistently underpredicts women's grades and overpredicts men's grades. Young women tend to receive higher college grades than young men with the same SAT scores (Bridgeman & Wendler, 1989). In addition, the Preliminary Scholastic Assessment Test (PSAT), which is used to distribute more than 14,000 scholarships in the United States, results in only 40 percent of the scholarships awarded to girls. However, girls consistently get higher grades on average than boys in both high school

FIGURE 27

Sample Form for Student Critique of Proficiency Test

Form number _____
Grade level _____

Tests are improved by field testing them. YOU, the test taker, are one of the most valuable sources for test improvement.

Please help us make this a fairer test by marking an X in a numbered box in response to each statement on the left. At the bottom of this sheet, you have a chance to give more detailed reactions in your own words.

Statements	Strongly disagree 1	Disagree 2	Neutral 3	Agree 4	Strongly agree 5
1. The test was fair as a minimum standard for graduation.	☐	☐	☐	☐	☐
2. The test items were clear in the way they were worded. (Please list below the number of any items that were unclear and explain why they were unclear.)	☐	☐	☐	☐	☐
3. The directions given were clear and complete.	☐	☐	☐	☐	☐
4. The test items were interesting.	☐	☐	☐	☐	☐
5. The pictures and diagrams were large enough.	☐	☐	☐	☐	☐
6. The printing was large enough and was spaced clearly.	☐	☐	☐	☐	☐
7. The test was administered clearly and carefully. (Did you know how much time you had left?)	☐	☐	☐	☐	☐
8. The atmosphere was conducive to test taking. (Was the room quiet?)	☐	☐	☐	☐	☐

General reaction/complaints: Please take a few minutes to describe your reactions to this test, referring to specific sections or questions on the test if you can.

_____

_____

From *Proficiency Assessment Handbook: Bias and Fairness in Proficiency Assessment* (Appendix M), produced by the California State Department of Education, 1979, Sacramento. Reprinted by permission.

and college, despite the fact that they score 50 to 60 points lower than boys on the PSAT and on the more advanced version of the test, the SAT. When one educational agency ceased to use this test in assigning scholarships, the percentage of girls who were awarded scholarships increased from 43 to 51 percent (Winerip, 1994). A study of college students found that a woman taking the same math course as a man in college and getting the same grade on average had a SAT score 35 points lower than the man (Wainer & Steinberg, 1990).

Studies also have found that on verbal test questions on the SAT, girls tend to do better on questions that are general and abstract and when questions deal with concepts and ideas rather than with facts and things

(Wendler & Carlton, 1987). The context in which the test question is placed influences how girls or boys will perform. When the context is science or sports, boys typically do better, but if the context is aesthetics, philosophical areas, or relationships, girls tend to do better (Rosser, 1989). Problems with unfamiliar content are more likely to be unanswered or solved incorrectly by girls.

Although most of these findings apply to U.S. students, or to students from other countries applying to U.S. colleges and universities, they would not necessarily bear the same results in other countries. However, each country should check its own selection examinations to determine if there is systematic bias against girls or any other subgroup and take steps to correct sources of bias.

Inequity Due to Language Limitations

Language can influence what students learn—or do not learn—and how they perform on examinations. Many developing countries are represented by several language groups, and many require a single language of instruction—different from many children's home language. This makes it more difficult for students to understand what is being taught; the problem is exacerbated when the teacher is not fluent in the language of instruction and, in some cases, not fluent in the students' home language. There is some evidence that these differences in language serve to disadvantage some students.

Issues of language deficiency are most evident when scoring essay or open-ended questions. There is a concern as to whether scoring guides can be designed so that markers can distinguish among problems that are as-

---

TABLE 3

Plots of Percent Correct Values on Math Subtest, by Subgroup

Subgroup I		Subgroup II		Subgroup III	
Percent correct value	Item number	Percent correct value	Item number	Percent correct value	Item number
1.0		1.0		1.0 — xx	9, 10
0.9 — x	9	0.9		0.9 — x	4
0.8		0.8		0.8 — x	1, 3
0.7		0.7		0.7 — xxx	2, 6, 8
0.6 — xx	3, 7	0.6 — x	9	0.6 — x	5
0.5 — xx	1, 5	0.5 — x	2	0.5 — x	7
0.4 — xxxx	2, 4, 6, 10	0.4 — xx	4, 6	0.4	
0.3		0.3 — xxx	1, 5, 10	0.3	
0.2		0.2 — xx	3, 7	0.2	
0.1 — x	8	0.1 — x	8	0.1	
0.0		0.0		0.0	
Mean=4.8 Standard deviation=2.04		Mean=3.3 Standard deviation=1.49		Mean=7.7 Standard deviation=1.64	

From *Proficiency Assessment Handbook: Bias and Fairness in Proficiency Assessment* (Appendix M), produced by the California State Department of Education, 1979, Sacramento. Reprinted by permission.

sociated with language deficiency, deficiency in the content area, or differences in students' responses simply because they are different or creative. Wolf and Reardon (1993, pp. 6, 10) provide examples of two students' responses to a story to demonstrate this point:

> "Jemo Shinda" is a short story by Hisaye Yammamoto. In this story, the author tells about the time when her brother was run over by a fast car. By doing that, she makes you see the roaring 20's were not fun and games for everybody.

> The author, her name is Hisaye Yammato (sic) tell how the rich shiney (sic) cars coming home full or partying and drinking, they ran over a boy so poor and so foreign he was no different from their flat driveways or soft grass. It makes me to know when Mr. Fitzgerald write about the roaring 20's, it is roaring like a hungry animal, not like singing.

Although the first response is adequate in grammar, punctuation, and accuracy of summary, the second, written by a student who is still learning English, is far more rich in metaphor and imagery and also more creative. Both passages convey that the students clearly understood the meaning of the story. Depending on the scoring criteria, however, the second response could fail to receive any points due to deficiencies in grammar, spelling, and punctuation.

Some of the potential for inequity due to language limitations could be overcome by using scoring criteria with multiple scales, such as grammar, punctuation, spelling, imagery, comprehension, communication, and creativity. It is important to make clear to students which criteria are being used to make judgments.

Inequities Due to Use of Multiple Standards

In some countries, several examining bodies may operate simultaneously. For example, one region in Pakistan has eight different examining boards, each with different grading standards. Students who live in the region with more lenient standards are more likely to be selected for the next higher level of education. In fact, a recent study of the effects of different standards revealed that students who were admitted to a university based on examinations given by the more lenient boards had a higher first-year failure rate than students from more rigorous boards (Punjab, 1992).

Steps to a Better Testing System

As with any major reform effort, changes made in a testing system should be accompanied by an ongoing formative evaluation of how the changes are being interpreted and implemented as they pass from central ministerial levels to classroom levels. This information should be distributed throughout the system, and appropriate corrections in the assessments should be made. Any major changes will require regular and advanced communications with the affected constituents, opportunities for their input and feedback, and plenty of lead time for all parties to adjust to the changes.

Although technical specialists are the professionals most likely to be involved in the day-to-day activities of testing reform, educational policymakers are the initiators and overseers of the process. The following is a checklist of steps that policymakers and technicians can use to guide them in imple-

Effective teaching helps children see the connections between new knowledge and what they already know. © Aga Khan Foundation/Jean-Luc Ray. Used by permission.

menting a high-quality testing system designed to enhance teaching and learning.

1. Form an oversight, advisory committee of representatives of various stakeholders including teachers, headmasters, inspectors, parents, curriculum specialists, teacher educators, and policymakers to review and advise on aspects of designing and implementing the testing system.

2. Arrange for testing staff and teachers to receive training in strategies for developing criterion-referenced tests and in using test formats such as performance tasks that promote good teaching and learning.

3. Review the curriculum and textbooks to ensure they are consistent with the principles of good teaching and learning. Make revisions where needed.

4. Revise examinations and develop or select tests for use in national assessment.

5. Pilot test new forms of assessment and revise them based on teachers' suggestions and pilot results.

6. Review test results and administration procedures to check for test bias.

7. Provide teachers with training and assistance in classroom assessment, instruction, and use of test results.

8. Provide advance notice on changes in examinations so that teachers, students, and parents will feel that they have had sufficient time to prepare for the examinations. Explain changes and provide concrete examples.

9. Develop booklets for teachers that describe what will be tested and how it will be tested and that provide suggestions for teaching.

10. Develop booklets for parents that explain proposed changes in the examinations and contain suggestions for how parents can help their children learn what will be measured on the examinations.

11. Develop booklets that students can use to prepare for selection examinations. All students should have equal access to these booklets. If there is a charge, it should be affordable for all parents.

12. Involve teachers in scoring essay tests, performance tasks, and open-ended questions.

13. Report test results on a timely basis, and provide teachers with nontechnical, easy-to-read reports that analyze students' problems and offer concrete suggestions for how to improve instruction.

14. Report assessment results in a way that acknowledges that results are a function of various factors other than schooling, such as parent income and education, geographic location, primary language, and opportunity to learn.

15. Make clear how the ministry of education is using test results to improve parts of the educational system, including

- the curriculum,
- textbooks and teacher guides,
- teacher training and staff development,
- technical assistance to schools and teachers, and
- follow-up research, including using teachers as researchers.

16. Try new tests (or performance tasks) once or twice in small-scale pilot activities, and use the information gathered in the pilot activities to make improvements in the tests and to give teachers, students, and parents feedback on how students are performing. At this stage, feedback should not identify specific schools, teachers, or students but should reflect general strengths and weaknesses and provide suggestions for improvement.

Tests are critical to how students view their educational experience. They are critical to schools as guides for improvement and to a nation because they measure educational accomplishment. Quality tests can help build a quality nation—and for that reason alone, they are worthy of the most careful attention from concerned educators.

APPENDIX A

Description of Classroom Assessment for Teachers

Excerpt from Namibia's Teachers' Guide to the Syllabus for Natural Science and Health Education, Grade 5

(This text was provided to teachers to encourage them to do more and better assessment.)

Assessment: More Than Just Examinations and Tests

Why Assess?

A purpose of our work as teachers is to find out if children are learning. We need to know if children are learning so we can determine if we need to change the ways we are teaching. We also do this to see if children are having problems learning. We find out by assessing if our teaching is helpful and if children are having problems learning. We assess in order to ensure that we help children learn.

Assessing learning and our teaching helps us know our learners and ourselves better. It prepares us for our discussions with parents, other teachers, and community members. It also prepares us for determining if learners are ready to move to other topics, skills, and concepts, or if they are ready to move to the next grade. Assessing is an essential part of our job as teachers.

What Do We Assess?

To find out if children are learning, we first need to know what we want them to learn. The themes and topics in the Syllabus provide a general idea of what we want children to learn. The learning objectives express in broad terms the desired outcomes of the learning process for the themes or topic area. The basic competencies are the essential and specific knowledge, skills, and attitudes that learners should acquire. They are stated in behavioral terms. They are the basis for assessing whether children are learning. For example, look at the section of the Syllabus on the next page.

In this example, we want learners to demonstrate a method for purifying dirty water, and we also want them to explain how water is made safe by boiling. In the first instance, we are expecting them to apply a process or procedure for filtering water. In the second instance, we are expecting them to understand the need for purifying water.

How Do We Assess Learning?

There are many ways to find out if children are learning what we want them to learn. As in the previous example, it is the basic competencies that should be assessed,

Theme/Topic	Learning Objectives	Basic Competencies
Water	The learning objectives for the theme "water" are to be achieved through practical experiences and investigations, whenever possible, so that learners will:	To demonstrate achievement of the learning objectives for "water" (by the acquisition of the related scientific knowledge, process skills, and attitudes), learners will be able to:
How to clean dirty water and purify contaminated water	■ apply a process for filtering dirty water ■ understand the need for purifying contaminated water by boiling	■ demonstrate at least one method of filtering dirty water ■ explain how water is made safe by boiling

and, if assessed, will tell teachers if children are learning. Some competencies are related to knowledge and understanding. Others are related to skills or attitudes. Knowledge and understanding are usually stated with action words such as explain, describe, name, or state. These can be assessed through written tests, quizzes, or assignments that ask the learners to explain or describe; or they can be assessed through asking the learners to orally explain, describe, name, etc.

You should try to be as creative as you can in assessing learning. Written tests and quizzes are not the only ways to assess knowledge and understanding. Remember, the method you use to assess also can be a useful way for children to learn. For example, let's say you are teaching the topic of clean water and you would like to know if the children are learning. You could divide the class into two teams.

Each team can make up 10 questions to ask the other group about what they are learning about clean water. Then each team can take turns asking their questions. The team with the most correct answers gets a treat from the other team. Another example might be to have the learners imagine that they are the mayor or headman of their town or village. As the mayor or headman, they are to write a public service announcement for the radio about the importance of clean water, how water in the town or village gets dirty, and ways to keep water clean. From these methods of assessment you can find out if children are learning what they are supposed to.

As mentioned before, some competencies relate to concrete, practical skills or to thinking skills. These kinds of competencies are usually written in terms of observe, collect, record, conclude, etc. They are not about explaining or describing how to do something. They are about actually doing or thinking through something. Assessing skills is a very important part of our job as teachers, but it can also be a very difficult part of our job. To assess skills, we must provide learners with opportunities to both develop the skills and to show us that they can do them. For example, let's say that we want learners to be able to observe, collect, and record data and to make conclusions about a water source. These are all very important skills in learning about science and health. A possible way to help children learn these skills and also to assess whether they can do them is to follow the following sequence of activities:

1. Take the learners to a local water source and ask them questions about what they see. Help them see that through observation we can learn a lot about a situation.

2. Show them how to record what they see in their notebooks.

3. Talk about making conclusions with them and ask them about what conclusions they would make about the purity of the water at this water source.

4. Then divide the class into smaller groups and ask each one to choose a different local water source. Ask each group to observe the water source, record their observations, and make written conclusions about the purity of the water. Also ask the groups to submit a brief report of this activity to you. Through the report and discussion with the learners, you can find out if they are learning the skills.

Still other competencies relate to attitudes. Attitudes such as willingness to work with other children, appreciation for the importance of clean water, and willingness to observe a situation and make conclusions are also very important competencies to assess. However, attitudes such as these are also difficult to assess. Probably the best way for a teacher to assess attitudes is to observe the learners closely. Through observation, it is possible to see if learners have the attitudes that we would like them to have. It is also possible to assess attitudes through having the learners do projects that would give you an indication of their attitude. For example, having the learners make a poster about the importance of clean water would help you to see if they really appreciate the importance of clean water. Another possible way of assessing attitudes is to spend some time with each learner and talk with him or her about the theme or topic at hand. Through the discussion, you will be able to assess the attitudes of the learner.

For more information about how to assess particular competencies, look at the suggestions provided in the assessment section for each objective discussed in this Teacher's Guide.

What Else Do We Assess?

As teachers, we also should be concerned about our teaching. How we are teaching will affect learning. So, we also should assess our teaching. To do this, it is best to have some basic standards or measures against which we can assess ourselves. For example, questions we could ask ourselves to determine how we are doing could include the following.

- Did I plan well for this lesson? (clear objectives for the lesson, appropriate materials/aids, well-prepared activities)

- Did I use information from my informal and formal continuous assessments to help plan the lesson?

- Did I establish a cooperative learning environment in the classroom? (learners worked together in groups, as appropriate; learners were encouraged to ask questions; learners were encouraged to assist one another; learners were interested in the lesson; learners were active)

- Did I communicate well with the learners? (concepts clearly stated, instructions clearly stated, asked questions to see if learners understood)

- Did I find out if any learners were having problems with the lesson? (asked questions to continually assess whether learners were having difficulty, observed for confused looks)

- Did I use appropriate teaching techniques? (good questions and examples, helpful teaching aids, appropriate language for the learners, not too much lecturing)

- Did I manage the class effectively? (handled administrative tasks smoothly, kept learners' interest, handled inattentive learners with care and understanding)

- Did I continually assess the lesson and make changes, as necessary? (modified the lesson if constrained by time or the difficulty of concepts for learners, assessed whether learners were learning, gave assistance to learners having problems)

How Often Do We Assess?

In order to find out if children are learning or having problems, we must assess often. Assessing often is called "continuous assessment." All assessment should be continuous.

Continuous assessment doesn't mean testing often. It means communicating with the learners often to find out if they are learning or having any problems. Tests are only one way to assess learners. Other ways include observing and listening to learners in group discussions, looking over the learners' homework books and in-class assignments, having competitive but fun games and observing participation, having a group of learners make a presentation to the class of what they have learned, and at the end of a class period asking learners to summarize what they have learned or having a brief chat with each learner. This kind of continuous assessment is usually informal. It is informal because it is not normally structured and systematic. It is also often based more on subjective feelings about the learner, and thus is not always an objective measure of progress or achievement. Nevertheless, it is a necessary part of our work in assessing. And, in borderline cases, it can provide the additional information needed to decide whether a learner passes.

However, continuous assessment also should be done in a formal way. That is, in addition to exams and tests, we can do the things mentioned above but in an objective, structured, and systematic way. The important thing with formal continuous assessment is that it is based on objective criteria of some kind. That is, we base our assessment method on observable, measurable, and specific standards. We use the marks from formal continuous assessment to determine an overall mark for the learner at the end of the term.

How Do We Provide Marks?

We all know that we must at some point provide marks for each learner. It is expected of us. However, providing marks can be a tricky business if we do not approach it objectively—that is, if we do not base the marks we provide on facts. Some teachers may give marks based on how they feel about a learner. We must strive to leave feelings out when giving marks.

One way to approach giving marks in an objective way is to decide while planning the lesson what will be assessed. This can be done by

1. reviewing the basic competencies for the theme or topic being taught and also the assessment sections in the Teacher's Guide for the theme or topic;

2. deciding how you will assess the basic competencies (i.e., what specific criteria you will use to make sure the learners have acquired the basic competencies and what method of assessment will be used); and

3. determining how many marks/points learners will get for addressing each criterion.

If you will be assessing knowledge-related competencies, you must determine the specific pieces of knowledge that learners must know. For example, let's say learners are to acquire the basic competencies as follows:

■ identify at least two ways one can get diarrhea and ways to prevent it, and

■ identify characteristics and causes of dehydration.

Then you must decide exactly what learners should identify. In this example you might decide that learners should be able to identify as three ways that one can get diarrhea:

1. drinking polluted water,

2. not washing their hands before eating, or

3. not washing fruits and vegetables with clean water.

You also might decide that if the learner can identify in writing two of these three then he or she would get 100 percent for this basic competency. The same would be true for the characteristics and causes of dehydration. You might decide that learners should be able to identify that (1) a child with dehydration has sunken in eyes that are dark and not healthy looking, (2) his or her skin is a bit like soft clay and when you pinch it stays pinched and doesn't go back to its normal color or shape, and (3) the dehydrated child has very dry lips. As far as causes of dehydration are concerned, you might decide that learners should be able to identify that diarrhea and the loss of fluids from the body causes dehydration as does vomiting. If the learners are able to identify all of these characteristics and causes, then they should get 100 percent for this basic competency.

If you want to assess skill competencies, the same procedure as above can be done. You just need to be sure what items you are looking for. For example, let's say that you are assessing the skill of observing a water source. You may look for the ability of the learner to (1) see more than just the water source, but everything around it as well, and (2) see how different things interact with or affect one another. So in this example you would be looking for two items. Two out of two possible would be 100 percent. One out of two possible would be 50 percent.

Please remember! The important thing about giving marks is that they should be based on objective criteria and not on your subjective feelings.

It is useful to base each of the marks you give on 100 percent. In this way you can easily find the average of the marks in order to come to a final mark at the end of the term. Remember also that the continuous formal assessment activities count for 80 percent of the final mark and the written tests and exams account for 20 percent of the final mark.

From *Teacher's Guide to the Syllabus* (Natural science and health education, grade five), developed by the National Institute for Educational Development, Namibia Ministry of Education and Culture, 1995, Windheck. Reprinted by permission.

APPENDIX B

Sample Performance Tasks, Open-Ended Questions, and Multiple-Choice Questions

Sample Performance Task in Science, Grade 8

(The following note is provided by the education agency to the teachers in the state.)

The following sample performance task represents a distinct departure from traditional large-scale assessment, in which there is minimal teacher involvement. This task is representative of only one of several types of performance tasks that may be used in the grade 8 science test. The task has two primary purposes. First, it is designed to gauge how well students can solve a real-world scientific problem in a laboratory setting. Students are required to develop their own hypothesis, design a method by which to test this hypothesis, and draw conclusions based on their observations and the information they have collected. Through these procedures students are given the opportunity to generate their own thinking about a scientific problem and to apply their own problem-solving abilities.

The second purpose of this task is to provide information about students' strengths and weaknesses when they are actively engaged in scientific problem solving. During this task the teacher is encouraged to facilitate students' successes by provoking their thinking, answering procedural questions, asking students to rethink a particular step in the process, and clarifying anything that is

unclear. The teacher's role, then, is to create a supportive classroom atmosphere that will encourage students to perform to their potential and to give their best effort to complete the task.

This task is designed to assess student performance in each of the following domains of the science assessment:

- acquiring and classifying scientific data and information
- communicating and interpreting scientific data and information
- solving problems—investigating
- solving problems—applying knowledge

Planning the Performance Task

As with a classroom laboratory investigation, all materials should be collected and organized prior to administering a performance assessment. For this sample task, teachers should plan to prepare anywhere from a minimum of five stations for the entire class to a maximum of one station for each student. A set of nondisposable materials will be needed for each station, and a set of disposable materials will be needed for each student. The disposable materials will be used by each student during the performance task and will have to be replaced. It is not necessary to separate students completely while they work. However, the room should be organized so that students can work quietly and independently.

This performance task is designed so that most students can complete it within a one-week period.

Before beginning a performance task in a laboratory, the teacher should review with students these standard safety rules:

- A laboratory is safe only if you treat laboratory work in a serious manner and follow safety guidelines.

- Handle glassware with care, and notify the teacher immediately if any glassware breaks.

- Wear goggles if you are told to do so.

- Return materials to the proper place, and clean up your working area.

Instructions for Sample Performance Task

Investigating the Absorbency of Paper Towels

Students will be given the following problem:

You work for a large restaurant. Your employer asks you to recommend a better brand of paper towel to use in the restaurant. Your first task is to figure out which of the three brands of paper towels is the most absorbent and to communicate your results to your employer. Your second task is to list other factors that you think should be considered before a new paper towel is selected for the restaurant.

Materials

At a station set up by the teacher, students will find two sets of materials: nondisposable and disposable. All the materials need to be ready before the students begin.

Nondisposable materials:

1 graduated cylinder

1 metric ruler

1 dropping pipette or eyedropper

1 pair of scissors

1 250 milliliter beaker or similar size container

1 balance scale

3 identical wide-mouth containers

1 clock or watch with a second hand

Disposable materials:

1 sheet each of three different brands of paper towels (labeled X, Y, and Z)

extra towels for cleanup

1 sheet of wax paper about 20 centimeters long

200 milliliters of water

Investigation

This task is designed to be completed in four parts. The instruction to the students as well as descriptions of successful responses are given below.

Part 1. Planning Your Investigation

(Parts 1 and 2 will be completed at the station.)

Plan an experiment that will enable you to show which brand of paper towel will absorb more water. Write a description of the procedure you will follow, and include the materials you plan to use. (You do not have to use all the materials at your station.)

Description of a Successful Response (Part 1)

The student's description of the procedure for the experiment is logical, ordered, and detailed enough to be easily replicated. In the design all relevant variables are tested and controlled. Materials for the investigation are chosen appropriately and listed accurately. The appropriate metric units are given.

Part 2. Conducting Your Investigation

When you have completed your plan, conduct the experiment. You may change your original plan as you work. Record your observations. After you conduct your experiment and record your observations, place all the nondisposable materials in a corner of the station and discard the disposable materials.

Description of a Successful Response (Part 2)

The student clearly and accurately records the data taken during the investigation. Data are clearly labeled and organized. The observations are complete and include data that can lead to further investigation.

Part 3. Communicating Your Results

Make a chart or graph that shows the result of your experiment.

Summarize the procedure you followed in your experiment, and discuss any changes you made in your plan. From the results you

obtained, state your conclusions about which paper towel is the most absorbent.

Description of a Successful Response (Part 3)

The student clearly communicates the data in an appropriate pictorial, graphic, or symbolic mode. Results of the investigation are well organized and labeled, and data can be easily interpreted.

The student's description of the procedure and the analysis of the data clearly follow the data and problem. The conclusion drawn is strongly supported and clearly communicated. Conclusions often acknowledge the limitations of methods used and the possible sources of error.

Part 4. Going Beyond Your Investigation

Discuss other factors that you think should be considered in order to select the overall best brand for the restaurant's use.

Description of a Successful Response (Part 4)

Other factors that might affect the choice of which paper towel is best to use, such as thickness, the price per package, or the amount per roll, are taken into consideration and discussed in a logical and comprehensive manner.

From *Texas Assessment of Academic Skills: 1990–1995 Science Objectives and Measurement Specifications, Tested at Grade 8*, developed by the Texas Education Agency, 1995, Austin.

Sample Performance Task in Mathematics

Comparing Supermarket Prices
Notes to the Teacher

Primary Focus

Mathematical application

Summary

How can you really tell which supermarket will save you the most money? By comparing prices at two supermarkets, students are to design and carry out a study to answer the question.

Curriculum Topics

Using computational skills such as integers, decimals, and fractions; understanding units of measurement; computing conversion between different units; gathering data, organizing data in tabular or graphic form; interpreting of data in problem solving; being able to write conclusions in clear narrative form.

Preparation

Some experience with graphs, tables, and comparisons; discussion of unit costs, average costs, and sales prices.

Information Needed

Location of stores and how to locate them.

Equipment Needed

Calculators, transparencies or posterboard, and markers

Sequence of In-Class Work and Out-of-Class Work (total time 2 weeks)

- 1–2 days: (in class) set the stage, discuss the problem, have students complete Part I individually,
- 1–3 days: (in class) set up groups and have each group develop final plan for preliminary grading, comments, and suggestions.
- 1–3 days: (out of class) collect data.
- 3–4 days: (in class) analyze data; prepare written report and oral presentation.
- 1–2 days: (in class) groups present orally in front of the class.
- 1 day: individuals do transfer task (Part III).

Techniques

- Suggest that students keep a log of individual work.
- You may wish to introduce the concept of a weighted average: should an item bought on a regular basis, such as bread or milk, have the same value in the calculations as an item that is rarely bought or a luxury item?
- The idea of a typical "market basket" can be introduced. Use a big folder in the classroom for the group work so that it is not lost between days, and the group can continue even if a member is absent.
- You may want to do the individual transfer task (Part III) in two days, de-

pending on the ability level and speed of the students.

- Other suggested comparisons that may be more relevant for students might include recordings, tapes, or fast foods.

- You may wish to make use of comparison tables published in consumer periodicals.

Suggested Topics for Discussion:

Fallacies used in misleading advertisements

Types of Reasoning Used

If this task is administered after students have studied the different types of logical reasoning, the task could be an excellent source of insight and an occasion for assessing their ability to make these distinctions. The examples of each type of reasoning in this task are clear and easily accessible.

1. Deductive—figuring out unit pricing and then comparing value based on price per unit is deductive reasoning.

2. Inductive—extending the pattern of findings to speculation about the prices of items not considered is inductive reasoning.

3. Statistical—using selected items that are believed to be representative of pricing policy of a particular store, then drawing conclusions about all prices in store based on the sample, is the method used in statistical reasoning.

4. Analogical—using similarities and differences between items, prices, and values is reasoning through analogy.

Student Task

Many local food markets claim to have the lowest prices. But what does this really mean? Does it mean that every item in the store is priced lower or just some of them? How can you really tell which supermarket will save you the most money? Your assignment is to design and carry out a study to answer this question.

Part I Beginning by Yourself

Design a Study

Design a study to determine which supermarket has cheaper prices. Describe your plan in a written report. Your report should answer the following questions:

1. What two food markets would you compare?

2. How would you compare the prices at the two stores? How would you select the products to be compared, and how would you record the comparisons?

3. How would you analyze the data to be collected in order to answer the research question?

Part II-A Group Work

Conduct a Study

The class will be formed into small research groups. You will become a member of a group of 3 or 4 students. You and the other members of your group will be required to hold two meetings during class time to compare the plans each of you developed and to develop a final plan for this assignment. Your plan must be designed to answer the three questions in Part I, and it should specify the responsibilities of each group member.

Your group will hand in your final plan for preliminary grading, comments, and suggestions before you carry it out.

Your group will carry out the plan, with each group member doing a separate part of the data collection and analysis. This will probably require two visits to the food markets you have chosen.

Each group will report separately on the project. Your final report should include the following information:

1. State the problem the research project was designed to solve

2. State how the data were collected. Include your specific role in collecting the data (who did what).

3. State how you analyzed the data. Explain why you chose the method of analysis selected. Include all of the analyses you did.

4. State your final conclusion. In other words, if someone asked you which supermarket has lower prices, how would you answer?

5. Include one or more graphic representations of your data to illustrate and support your final conclusions.

Each group will report orally on their project. The presentation should make use of all the information included in the final written report.

Part II-B Group Work

1. Suppose that you are managers of the store that your group found to have higher prices. Write a letter to your group critiquing the study or defending your pricing policies.

2. Advertising is supposed to tell us when and where we can get the best price for things we need and want. Consider the following advertisements:

SUPER SALE! PRICES REDUCED 50%!!!

ON WEDNESDAYS ONLY, TAKE ANOTHER 10% OFF THE SALE PRICE, FOR A TOTAL SAVINGS OF 60%!!!!

FOUR OUT OF FIVE, 80%, OF DENTISTS who recommend that you chew gum RECOMMEND NEPTUNE GUM !!!

What is wrong with these ads? Write an essay on how the stores are trying to mislead the consumers, and what steps consumers can take to avoid being misled. Use examples from your personal experience to support the points you make.

Part III Finishing by Yourself

There are many other stores that can be compared using approaches such as you used with the supermarket price comparison. For example, you might want to compare two clothing stores. The task that follows is based on this idea.

Assume that you are a newspaper writer and your editor has asked you and another reporter to do an article comparing two clothing stores—Habib's and Allen's. You are going to write the part of the article dealing with price comparisons.

Read and answer the questions below:

1. What information do you need from Habib's and Allen's in order to do the

price comparison? Be very specific: make a list that is complete enough for your assistant so that he can go to each store and get the information for you.

2. Now assume that your assistant has let you down. He took your instructions and the pay advance you gave him and never returned. You now have only a half hour to meet your editor's deadline for the article, so you have to use a newspaper ad for the stores as your only source of information. Now what do you do?

Prepare an analysis of the price information in the newspaper article, designed to answer the question—which store has the lower clothing prices? Attach your computation to your final response. You may use your calculator, but attach and label any numbers you compute that you use in the chart.

Your answer to question 2 should consist of one or more charts, graphs or tables that you feel help answer the question "Which clothing store has the lowest prices?" Remember, you are not concerned about quality in your analysis. Try to design one or more charts, graphs, or tables that are very informative about the question of which store has the lower prices and that are also clear and simple enough for the newspaper reading public to understand. Be sure to label your work so that it is self-explanatory to those who read the newspaper.

3. Write a paragraph for the newspaper article that addresses the question of which store has the lowest prices. In writing this paragraph, remember who your audience is and what you are trying to communicate to them.

From *Toward a New Generation of Student Outcome Measures: Connecticut's Common Core of Learning Assessment*, by J.B. Baron et al., 1989. Reprinted by permission.

Sample of Open-Ended and Multiple-Choice Questions Testing Communications in English in Adult Basic Education

Reading and Responding to Factual Texts

Example Texts for Reading

Factual texts are formal, expository texts that provide information, usually for study purposes. They often have an impersonal and objective tone. They may include graphics to put across some of the information. They may contain some terms specific to the subject or topic. Examples are selected extracts of chapters or articles from text books, reference books, newspapers, magazines, or contents pages.

Performance Outcomes

The candidates should be able to:

- recognize the main purpose of a specific factual text, its intended audience (who is it for), and likely source (where it comes from).

- use the most appropriate reading strategies to suit the text type and the task (such as skimming, scanning, reading for detail, predictive reading, guessing words from context, or breaking down words).

- show understanding of a factual text by responding to tasks that test comprehension (by answering questions such as who, what, where, when, why and how).

- identify words and phrases common to factual texts (for example, use of present tense, verbs as nouns, passives, adverbial and adjectival phrases, referencing, conditionals, there is/there are, and use of the verb "to be").

- respond to both textual and visual features (titles, subtitles, paragraphs, tables, graphs, charts, pie charts, and typeface) in order to understand the texts.

- understand techniques of organizing information in factual texts (introduction of topic, definitions, descriptions, classification, explanation and examples, comparing and contrasting, and cause and effect).

- identify any missing or misleading information.

- relate the contents of the text to personal experience or prior knowledge of the subject of the text.

Sample Task

Read the following factual text and answer the following questions.

One of South Africa's Biggest Killers

1 Tuberculosis (TB) is a very dangerous sickness. It usually attacks the lungs, although it sometimes attacks the brain or the bones. TB can be passed on to other people very easily. Every day, more than 10 people die of TB in South Africa. It is time to stop this killer disease.

2 200 years ago, there was no TB in South Africa. It is thought that the

English miners brought the disease here, where it spread very quickly in the mines.

3 Anyone can catch TB. However, people who are weak or in poor health catch TB more quickly. This means that in places where there is unemployment, no money to buy food, overcrowded houses, and bad living conditions, more people get TB. Only babies up to a month old can get BCG injection to prevent them from catching TB.

4 Many people do not know that they are suffering from TB. If they have TB they will show signs such as coughing all the time or coughing up blood; not wanting to eat; chest pains; night fever; or feeling sick, tired, or weak. If people think they have TB, they should go for a check-up and a chest X-ray. TB patients can be cured if they get treatment early.

5 TB is treated with injections and pills. TB sufferers also need proper food and rest. Education can also help people to understand more about TB and how to cure it. However, unless the government stops the root causes of TB, it will continue to be a killer disease in this country.

Questions on "One of South Africa's Biggest Killers"

1. What kind of writing is this?
   a. a story
   b. a poem
   c. a magazine article
   d. a play

2. Where can you often see this kind of writing?
   a. in a newspaper or a magazine
   b. on a street poster
   c. in a children's book
   d. in a diary

3. What is the goal of the writer?
   a. to tell us how to get a better house
   b. to educate us about TB in South Africa
   c. to tell us where we can go to get treatment for TB
   d. to make us laugh about TB

4. Why did the writer use the drawing [not shown in this example] in the title?

   _____

   _____

5. What is each paragraph about? Write the paragraph number that matches the sentence:

   Signs that you may have TB
       paragraph _____

   What TB is, where it is found in your body, and how many people die from it
       paragraph _____

   Where TB first came from
       paragraph _____

   Treatment for TB
       paragraph _____

   How TB spreads & which people can catch it
       paragraph _____

6. Fill in this table about TB in note form, using few words.
   What TB is _____
   Where TB is found in the body _____

Where TB first came from _____
Who catches TB more easily _____
What helps TB to spread (give one more reason) _____
Signs of TB (give three more) _____
Treatment for TB (give three) _____
How to prevent TB in babies _____

7. Match the words and phrases that mean nearly the same thing

not strong	disease
sickness	no work
overcrowded houses	weak
patient	bad living conditions
treatment	sufferer
unemployment	cure

8. Write the word or words in paragraph 2 that tell us that some information is not true or sure.

_____

9. In the last paragraph, what are the "root causes" of TB? The writer does not tell us clearly what they are. Write one root cause of TB that you can think of.

_____

10. In this writing, does the writer show personal feelings or opinions?
Yes___   No___
Write one phrase from the text that tells you this.

_____

11. What question do you want to ask about TB that is not answered in this writing? Give one more question.
example Where can I go to get treatment for TB?

_____

12. Do you think this is a good piece of writing?
Yes___   No___
Give a reason for your answer.

_____

From *Adult Basic Education User's Guide, Communications in English Examinations Syllabus*, produced by the Independent Examinations Board, 1994, Johannesburg, South Africa.

Sample Multiple-Choice Science Items Testing Conceptual and Thematic Understanding, Grade 8

1. The life span of a certain mammal is about 75 years. At conception, it weighs only a fraction of a gram. After birth, it begins eating, and gains weight steadily until it reaches a maximum weight of 80 kilograms. The mammal's weight comes mostly from atoms of carbon, hydrogen, and oxygen, along with a few other elements. The atoms are arranged into groups, called molecules. The most plentiful molecule in the mammal's body is water. Proteins, lipids (fats), and carbohydrates are also important molecules. Where did the carbon, hydrogen, and oxygen atoms in the mammal's body come from before the mammal used them for growth?
   a. They came from the mammal's habitat.
   b. They were inherited from the mammal's parents.
   c. They were manufactured in the mammal's body.
   d. They were extracted from the atmosphere.

2. The energy that the mammal uses to join atoms together, to move, and to produce body heat is
   a. generated as the mammal digests its food.
   b. generated when the mammal's heart pumps blood to the cells.
   c. generated by the muscles when the mammal exercises.
   d. not generated by any of the methods above.

3. When the mammal breathes, it takes in oxygen and gives off carbon dioxide. This carbon dioxide
   a. cannot be used by any other living thing.
   b. is converted into oxygen by sunlight.
   c. will help reduce global warming.
   d. can be used by other living things.

4. When the mammal dies, most of the atoms in its body
   a. will eventually become part of the rock cycle.
   b. will eventually be used by other living things.
   c. will be lost through condensation.
   d. will be converted directly into energy.

5. The energy that the mammal uses for its daily functions
   a. will be recycled into food energy by plants.
   b. will be stored in the habitat as kinetic energy.
   c. will be converted into heat and warm the environment.
   d. will be stored in the habitat as potential energy.

From *Preliminary Edition. Survey of Academic Skills—Science* (California Assessment Program), produced by the California State Department of Education, 1991, Sacramento. Used by permission.

APPENDIX C
Sample Essay Test

Text and Prompt for History Writing Test

(This is an example of a writing prompt that involves students in working from original speeches and that tells them what is expected of them in their essays. The specifications for this test are in Chapter 4.)

Directions: As Abraham Lincoln and Stephen Douglas campaigned for the office of U.S. Senator from Illinois, they held seven joint debates throughout the state. Read the following passages to understand as well as possible what Lincoln and Douglas discussed in one of their debates.

Stephen A. Douglas

Mr. Lincoln tells you, in his speech made at Springfield, before the Convention which gave him his unanimous nomination, that

"A house divided against itself cannot stand."

"I believe this government cannot endure permanently, half slave and half free."

"I do not expect the Union to be dissolved, I don't expect the house to fall; but I do expect it will cease to be divided."

"It will become all one thing or all the other."

That is the fundamental principle upon which he sets out in this campaign. Well, I do not suppose you will believe one word of it when you come to examine it careful-ly and see its consequences. Although the Republic has existed from 1789 to this day, divided into Free States and Slave States, yet we are told that in the future it cannot endure unless they shall become all free or all slave. For that reason, he says, that they must be all free. He wishes to go to the Senate of the United States in order to carry out that line of public policy, which will compel all the States in the South to become free. How is he going to do it? Has Congress any power over the subject of slavery in Kentucky, or Virginia, or any other State of the Union? You convince the South that they must either establish slavery in Illinois, and in every other Free State, or submit to its abolition in every Southern State, and you invite them to make a warfare upon the Northern States in order to establish slavery, for the sake of perpetuating it at home. Thus, Mr. Lincoln invites, by his proposition, a war of sections, a war between Illinois and Kentucky, a war between the Free States and the Slave States, a war between the North and the South, for the purpose of either exterminating slavery in every Southern State.... (Note: Lincoln text included in original test.)

History Writing Prompt

Imagine that it is 1858 and you are an educated citizen living in Illinois. Because you are interested in politics and always keep yourself well informed, you make a special trip to hear Abraham Lincoln and Stephen Douglas debating during their campaigns for the State seat representing Illinois. After the debates you return home, where your cousin asks you about some of the problems that are facing the United States at this time.

Write an essay in which you explain the most important ideas and issues your cousin should understand. Your essay should be based on two major sources: (1) the general concepts and specific facts you know about American history, and especially what you know about the history of the Civil War; and (2) what you have learned from the readings. Be sure to show the relation among your ideas and facts.

From the *National Center for Research on Evaluation, Standards, and Student Testing (CRESST) Performance Assessment Models: Assessing Content Area Explanations* (CSE Technical Report Series), by E.L. Baker et al., 1992, Los Angeles, CA: CRESST. © 1992 by The Regents of the University of California and supported under the Office of Educational Research and Improvement, U.S. Department of Education. Reprinted by permission.

APPENDIX D
Sample Marking Guides

Tips for Teachers and a Checklist for Grading Listening and Speaking Tasks

(This text was included in a booklet prepared for adult basic education teachers in South Africa to inform them of a new system for assessing and certifying adult students.)

Tips for Teachers

The notes and the assessment checklist that follow may be helpful to you in grading a specific listening and speaking task, or as pointers to ongoing assessment of listening and speaking during a course. You may feel that you already have developed your own particular assessment methods in line with your own particular course requirements; our tips are not intended to replace these, and you can feel free to ignore this section of the guide if you like.

Keeping a Reliable Standard

It is important to try to keep the same standard when you are formally grading students on a particular task. It is all too easy to let your standards drift, so that the students who are graded at the end of the session get higher marks than those who are graded at the beginning. Or your standards can shift from one session to the next, if you are grading a few students each session.

It is not a good idea to grade students while they are doing the task—it makes them nervous. You should grade the student immediately after the task is completed, before the next student's turn.

In real life students will have to communicate in English with first-language users of English as well as second language users of a local variety of English. The grading should take into account how well the student communicates with both these groups.

You should try to make sure the conditions are the same for each rating session, such as the same room, quiet environment, same amount of time given to each student, and same level of language used by the assessor.

Making the Assessment a Pleasant Experience

Plenty of practice sessions on a variety of listening and speaking tasks (such as the ones given in this user guide) should help reduce nervousness. Practice sessions with the whole class are fine, but the formal grading on a particular task should be done privately with each student. It is a good idea for each student to have some practice with private grading sessions as well.

161

The student should not be cut off short when the time is up but should be allowed to finish in a dignified way. Thank the student and finish the session in a friendly, informal way. The student should always leave the session feeling it was a pleasant experience.

If a student is clearly not coping and the assessment is becoming embarrassing, do not leave the student to flounder through the whole task or for the whole time available. Find a pleasant, tactful way to allow the student to abandon the task (such as by asking one or two very simple questions or reverting to mother tongue) and ease out of the assessment.

General Performance Assessment

The comments above apply to assessing a specific task. Assessment of students' general performances throughout a course will take into account how they have dealt with specific tasks. In grading students on general performance, however, teachers can also bring in other factors. Teachers can take note of students' general speaking and listening behavior in class: For example, how well does a student work with others in a group? Does he or she take an active part in group discussions in English? Does he or she ask questions from the teacher or from classmates for clarification? How does a student perform when asked to read out loud in class? At times during a course, or at the end of a course, it is worth sitting back and thinking about a student's general progress in listening and speaking in English. This kind of reflection on a student can help you decide on a final course mark for oral work.

Using a Checklist

We have put together a checklist of listening and speaking skills that you might want to use to help you assess your learners. The checklist is based on assessment criteria for and comments on the Merit, Credit, and Threshold grades of the different aspects of speaking and listening skills.

The checklist is a tool that you can use or not as you like. It does not add anything new to what we have already said in earlier sections. It is simply a different way of organizing the assessment criteria for those who might want more detailed guidance on assessing speaking and listening.

There are several ways in which you can use the checklist. You could use it when you are grading students on a particular task; in this case, you could put a tick in the block that best describes the student's performance according to each of the features in the checklist such as grammar, checking on own and other person's understanding, etc.

When you have finished the blocks, you can check to see if the student achieved mostly Merits, Credits, or Thresholds. This will help you to decide whether the student will get an overall Merit, Credit or Threshold grading.

The checklist is also useful for classroom practice. You can get the students to grade one another on one feature at a time and discuss their gradings versus yours. You can also use the checklist in practice sessions on different assessment tasks and discuss gradings with students. In this way you can help students to improve their performance because they know what features need improvement.

Although the checklist separates out various skills involved in listening and speaking, it is important to remember that in the end a teacher or examiner can only make an overall judgment on a candidate's general oral performance. You will find that some of the categories apply more to speaking, and some more to listening and understanding, and some apply to both. Most students probably will be able to follow and understand speech better than they can use it. The same comments we made about the assessment criteria apply here as well: that is, that the checklist is given to help you make an overall judgment and that it is not always possible to assess all the aspects given in the checklist in any one task.

Assessment Criteria

Speaking and listening performances will be assessed as how well candidates meet the following criteria:

- overall comprehension of the speaking and listening interaction
- achievement of main purpose of interaction

- appropriate use of voice (pronunciation, stress, pace, volume)
- appropriate use of body language (gesture, facial expression, etc.)
- appropriate use of language (grammar, vocabulary)
- fluency (control of speech, flow)
- knowing and using conventional patterns and routines of communication (e.g., greeting and leave taking conventions, how job interview, speeches or telephone inquiries usually happen, etc.)
- checking own and other people's understanding of the interaction while it is happening
- appropriate use of formal or informal language to suit the purpose of the interaction and the status, role, and feelings of the other parties in the interaction
- managing and maintaining the interaction
- detecting values, bias, hidden messages, and incomplete information
- making a judgment on whether the process of interaction succeeded

CHECKLIST FOR ASSESSING LISTENING AND SPEAKING TASKS

	Merit	Credit	Threshold
1. Overall comprehension of formal speech or interaction	Candidate understands sympathetic local speaker on familiar topic fairly well; follows with difficulty rapid conversation between speakers of English as a first language.	Candidate understands sympathetic local speaker on familiar, everyday simple topic (speaking slowly) fairly well, but needs some repetition and explanation.	Candidate has difficulty in following sympathetic local speaker, even on familiar topic; follows only everyday social interaction and limited, routine topics.
2. Achievement of main purpose of interaction	Candidate expresses and understands main ideas and/or feelings clearly and communication achieves its full purpose.	Candidate expresses and understands main ideas and/or feelings well enough for communication to succeed in its main purpose.	Candidate does not express and understand main ideas and/or feelings well enough for communication to succeed in its main purpose, although there is some evidence that most obvious points have been grasped.
3. Voice (e.g., pronunciation, stress, pace, volume, etc.)	Candidate is fairly easy for sympathetic local listener to understand; mother tongue influence on candidate's speech still obvious but does not interfere with understanding.	Candidate is fairly easy for sympathetic local listener to understand, but listener has to concentrate and does not always understand everything.	Candidate is difficult for sympathetic local listener to understand, candidate must frequently be asked to repeat.
4. Body language	Not disturbing to sympathetic listener and sometimes used effectively to support communication.	Occasionally disturbing to sympathetic listener but does not significantly interfere with communication.	Disturbing to sympathetic listener and interferes with communication.

(continued)

	Merit	Credit	Threshold
5. Language (grammar and vocabulary)	Candidate makes some common mistakes, but these do not impair understanding of sympathetic local listener. Candidate attempts more complicated structures, shows inventiveness where correct structure is not mastered. Attempts more adventurous vocabulary than minimum required for task. Sometimes has to use round-about paraphrase.	The gist of candidate's speech can be understood by sympathetic local listener, but details may be unclear. Candidate may occasionally be asked to repeat. Candidate uses basic structures fairly accurately but common mistakes are quite frequent. Candidate occasionally tries more complicated structures. Uses ordinary vocabulary required for task reasonably accurately but often has to use paraphrase.	Candidate uses only basic structure and telegraphic forms; language is sometimes fragmented and inaccurate. Candidate is difficult for even a sympathetic local listener to understand; candidate must frequently be asked to repeat. Uses only basic vocabulary and some stock phrases; sometimes misuses words. Candidate's limited vocabulary makes conversation quite difficult.
6. Fluency	Candidate is sometimes hesitant, needs occasional prompting. Pauses and breaks are not seriously disturbing to sympathetic listener; speech occasionally flows easily.	Candidate is quite often hesitant, needs fair amount of prompting and encouragement. Some awkward breaks and pauses occur in interaction.	Candidate is frequently hesitant, needs prompting often. Responses are limited and do not offer more than minimum information. Candidate needs a lot of prompting.
7. Knowing and using conventional patterns and routines of communication (e.g. conventions for telephone inquiries, formal speeches, greeting and leave taking, confirming arrangements, job interview conventions, etc.)	Candidate generally follows expected patterns and routines of communication.	Candidate generally follows expected patterns and routines of communication; occasionally uses unexpected or strange patterns but these do not seriously disturb sympathetic local listener.	Candidate does not use or misuses expected patterns.

[continued]

	Merit	Credit	Threshold
8. Checking own and other person's understanding	Candidate reacts to clear signals that misunderstanding is arising, asks questions and explains, checks that critical information is reasonably well understood. Recognizes that misunderstanding has occurred and tries to resolve it. This may or may not be successful.	Where there are clear signals that misunderstanding is arising, candidate grapples with problem but is unable to resolve it.	Candidate allows misunderstandings to continue/is not aware of misunderstandings.
9. Using appropriate language according to purpose and situation of interaction (where the interaction takes place, the relationship between participants, their roles and feelings) (e.g., ceremonial, formal, informal, friendly situations)	Candidate uses basic, neutral, polite forms, terms of address and tone of voice when in doubt; uses more formal or less formal language appropriate to situation but does not have great range of variations.	Candidate uses basic, neutral polite forms, terms of address and tone of voice for most interactions; sometimes uses more formal or less formal language appropriately for obviously more formal or less formal situations. Candidate is a bit hesitant when outside the basic, neutral polite range.	Candidate uses language inappropriately, or does not distinguish between formal/informal, or uses the same forms, terms of address and tone of voice for all situations even when clearly inappropriate.

(continued)

	Merit	Credit	Threshold
10. Managing & maintaining interaction (e.g., taking turns, introducing new topics, being assertive, being sympathetic, making encouraging noises)	Candidate manages and maintains interaction well when topic is relatively pleasant and fairly familiar. Candidate has some simple strategies when faced with aggression, intolerance or uncertainty, but shows some loss of control in these circumstances. Parties feel satisfied that the interactive process is working.	Candidate manages and maintains interaction well enough for interaction to proceed, as long as topic is relatively pleasant and fairly familiar. Can recognize but cannot cope with aggression, intolerance or uncertainty. Parties feel reasonably satisfied with the interaction, but there are occasional frustrations.	Candidate does not maintain conversation well enough for interaction to proceed. Candidate needs substantial support from other party; parties feel frustrated by interaction.
11. Detecting values, bias, hidden messages, concealment of information	Candidate detects most of the obvious examples and sometimes more subtle examples.	Candidate detects some obvious examples.	Candidate deals with surface meaning only.
12. Making a judgement on how well the interaction went	Candidate makes an accurate judgement on how the interaction went.	Candidate makes a fairly accurate judgement on how the interaction went, although the teacher and the candidate may disagree on some aspects.	While candidate might be aware of the failure of interaction, judgement on how it went is often confused, and teacher and candidate disagree.

From *Adult Basic Education User's Guide, Communications in English Examinations Syllabus*, produced by the Independent Examinations Board, 1994, Johannesburg, South Africa.

Sample Writing Prompt and Holistic and Analytic Guides for Scoring Essays

(This sample shows two approaches to scoring essays.)

Student Writing Prompt

The principal in your school has said that you have permission to take a fieldtrip in the spring. The principal has asked you to make suggestions about where to go on the trip. Select a place that your class would like to visit for a day. Write a note to the principal. Give the name of the place you have picked. Tell the reasons you think it is a good place for a fieldtrip.

Holistic Scoring Guide

Mark of 4 (highest mark)

Writer does all or most of the following:

1. Makes a decision about where to go. (Can give two places if support is shown for both.) Is likely to imply or state educational as well as recreational values of trip. May add details for planning trip. May make case for other students as well as for self.

2. Organizes details in some clear fashion to convince reader. Free of irrelevant details. Clear, fully developed paragraphs.

3. Shows superior command of language structure and vocabulary.

4. Shows superior grasp of spelling and mechanics. Reader proceeds rapidly. (Is not held up by inability to decipher handwriting, spelling, or sentence breaks and endings.)

Mark of 3

Writer does all or most of the following:

1. Makes a decision about where to go. Is likely to imply educational as well as recreational values of trip. May add details for planning trip. Less developed. Fewer details. May have some beginning of personal memories.

2. Organizes details, although reasons for trip not as fully developed. Linkage between sentences less strong.

3. Shows adequate command of language structure and vocabulary.

4. Shows adequate working grasp of spelling and mechanics. Reader proceeds rapidly. Only unfamiliar words are misspelled.

Mark of 2

Writer does all or most of the following:

1. Makes a decision about where to go. Justification is scanty or likely to be lost in personal reminiscence. Less awareness of other children. Personal memories and satisfactions likely to dominate composition.

2. Shows minimal organization. Few real linkages between sentences. Little development. Likely to be short.

3. Shows some command of language structure and vocabulary, but sentences are sometimes unclear, and meaning is

sometimes not immediately apparent to reader.

4. Shows sufficient grasp of spelling and mechanics for communication. Readers may be held up by confusing sentences and sentence parts. Many misspellings on familiar as well as unfamiliar words.

Mark of 1

Writer does all or most of the following:

1. Makes no decision or makes a decision but makes no case; for example, "It would be fun." May get lost in personal reminiscence.

2. Shows no apparent organization. Lack supporting detail. Mixes in irrelevant detail.

3. Lacks command of language structure and vocabulary to convey meaning.

4. Lack sufficient grasp of spelling and mechanics for adequate communication. Reader cannot understand because of confusing syntax and misspellings.

ANALYTIC SCORING GUIDE

Subscore Area	High (3)	Middle (2)	Low (1)
Content			
Ideas	Makes a decision about where to go. (Can give two places if support is shown for both.) Is likely to imply or state educational as well as recreational values of trip. May add details for planning trip. Makes the case for other students as well as for self. Makes a strong case to persuade the principal.	Makes a decision about where to go. May emphasize solely personal reasons (or stress personal more than educational reasons).	Makes no decision or makes a decision but does not make a strong case for it. May get lost in personal reminiscences.
Organization	The details are organized in a clear fashion to convince reader—a beginning, a middle, and an end. Free of irrelevant details. Clear paragraphing.	Less clear cut organization. Fewer details to support position. May not place strongest point in prominent position. Sentences may not always follow logically from previous sentence. May have some irrelevant details.	No visible organizational scheme. Lacks supporting details. Mixes in many irrelevant details.
Mechanics			
Syntax	Sentences are clear and unambiguous. Occasional run-ons, and few, if any, fragments.	Sentences are basically clear. Requires occasional rereading of a sentence. Some run-ons and/or fragments.	Reader has difficulty deciphering meaning of sentences. Many run-ons and/or fragments. Omits words or sentence parts.
Usage/word choice	Generally uses standard English (subject-verb agreement; case and reference of pronouns). Does not depend on slang.	Some errors in standard English (subject-verb agreement; case and reference of pronouns). May use slang, but not heavily dependent on it.	Does not use standard English (many errors in subject-verb agreement; case and reference of pronouns).

(continued)

ANALYTIC SCORING GUIDE (continued)

Subscore Area	High (3)	Middle (2)	Low (1)
Punctuation/ capitalization	Begins and ends sentences correctly, but they include some run-ons. Capitalizes proper nouns and "I." Uses commas in a series.	May occasionally fail to capitalize some proper nouns and "I"; may occasionally begin or end sentence incorrectly.	Lacks sure knowledge of what to capitalize and punctuate.
Spelling	Spells commonly used words correctly most of the time. When words are misspelled, they closely approximate correct spelling.	May misspell (more frequently) common words as well as "demons." Some phonetic spelling.	Many misspellings. Often does not appropriate correct spelling of word.

From the *Proficiency Assessment Handbook*, produced by the California State Department of Education, 1979, Sacramento. Used by permission.

APPENDIX E

Sample Test-Item Specifications

Sample Item Specifications for Environmental Education, Grades 10–12

Scientific Method

General Description

When given brief, previously unseen accounts of the research activity of natural and physical scientists, students will answer questions that are keyed to the accounts by selecting for each question the concept in the scientific method that is illustrated.

Sample Item

Directions: Read the following account of scientific research and answer the questions which follow it. The number of each question refers to the underlined part of the account that has the same number. For each question write the letter of the correct answer on the answer sheet.

Pasteur knew that people could be immunized against smallpox and (1) asked himself if cattle could be protected against anthrax in the same way. He took some anthrax germs and kept them cold and unfed until they were weak, then first injected a couple of sheep with these weakened germs. The sheep came down with only a very mild case of the usually deadly disease.

After a few days Pasteur gave these same sheep a shot of fresh, potent anthrax germs that would ordinarily kill a sheep within three days. The animals did not get sick.

The public was skeptical. (2) The possibility remained that Pasteur had made some kind of error or that the test sheep were unusually healthy animals. Would the vaccine still work if a large number of cows as well as sheep were tested? A public demonstration was set up. The study was done with (3) animals receiving the vaccine before getting the dangerous dose of anthrax germs and 25 others receiving only the dangerous germs. After three days all of the vaccinated animals were (4) healthy, but the other animals were almost all dead from anthrax. Pasteur's initial success with the vaccine was upheld.

1. When Pasteur asked himself if cattle could be protected against anthrax in the same way that humans can be protected against smallpox, he was thinking about a/an _____.
   a. fair sample
   b. replication
   c. measurement
   d. hypothesis

Rules for How the Question/Problem Is to Be Worded (Stimulus Attributes)

1. The stimulus part of an item will consist of the following two components:

   a. An account, in 15 sentences or less, that presents a sequence of research activity of one or more physical scientists. The account and the activity it describes will not have been studied before by the students. In the accounts, 3 to 5 sentences or phrases will be numbered and underlined. The numbers will start with (1) in the first account and run consecutively through the last numbered part in the last account. Two separate phrases may have the same number if they illustrate one term and if they are not separated by other underlined material. For example, see (4) in the sample item.

   b. A set of at least three questions numbered to correspond with the underlined portions of the account. Questions that deal with two separate phrases, as in (4) of the second paragraph below, will be so labeled.

2. The accounts will deal with the range of activities that researchers in the natural and physical sciences engage in while studying and explaining natural phenomena. Accounts may be adapted from biographies of scientists, histories of science, introductions to scientific method and philosophy of science, and science textbooks. They will be rewritten, if necessary, so that the wording does not specifically cue or eliminate any of the response alternatives. For example, the final word in the Pasteur account should not be "confirmed" if the term "confirmation" appears as a distracter in any item.

3. A question will be any declarative sentence in this form:
   (Material in the numbered and underlined part of the account) (was or were) (optional verb) (optional articles), such that terms will meaningfully and correctly complete the statement if inserted in the blank. For the parts numbered (2), (3), and (4) in the sample item, the following are examples:

   (2) That Pasteur had made an error and that the test sheep were unusually healthy animals _____.

   (3) The presence of the vaccine in one group and its absence in the other was a/an/the _____.

   (4) (Refers to two separate phases in the account) The health of the two groups of animals after they had received the dangerous germs and was a/an/the _____.

   A selection of articles is included so as not to tip off the correct response through article-noun compatibilities.

4. The test will include at least two accounts and at least eight concepts.

5. The accounts will be adapted to read at no higher than a 10th grade reading level.

Rules for How the Student Is to Respond (Response Attributes)

1. Students will respond by selecting one of four multiple choice alternatives.

Alternatives will be taken from the terms supplied.

2. The correct response will be the term whose meaning is exemplified or illustrated by the sentence. A good grade level source on scientific method will be the authoritative source of meanings.

3. Distracters (wrong answers) will be randomly selected from the remaining terms supplied with the following exception: a number of terms are either partial synonyms or can be illustrated by the same sentence or phrase (e.g., hypothesis-deduction-prediction; theory-explanation). When one of these terms is the correct response, none of the other similar terms will be used as distracters. This practice will ensure that there is only one correct response in the given set of response choices.

Specification prepared by IOX Assessment Associates, Los Angeles, CA. Used by permission.

Sample Specification for English-Listening Comprehension, Grade 1

Objective

Given a set of commands, such as "stand up," "walk slowly," "turn left," etc., the student will respond to the commands.

Administration

- Individually administered.
- Each student will have three minutes to respond to the command given.
- Each student must respond to five commands.

Scoring

After the student completes the task, evaluate the student's performance using the following three criteria. Check "yes" or "no" for each criterion.

Criteria

1. Responded correctly to the five commands.
2. Responded in the given time.
3. Demonstrated confidence.

Teacher Instructions

Say the commands very clearly and slowly, then say:

Today, I am going to ask you to do a few things for me. Listen carefully and then do as I say.

Stimuli

The commands will include
1. sit down
2. put up your right hand
3. open your mouth
4. touch your left ear
5. stand up
6. show your teeth
7. jump to the right
8. close the door
9. jump to the left
10. put your hands on your knees
11. walk slowly
12. stand on one foot
13. walk quickly
14. draw a line on the chalkboard

From *National Curriculum Centre/Continuous Assessment Unit, EPMT Project*, developed by the Swaziland Ministry of Education, 1992, Mbabane. Adapted by permission.

Sample Specification for Mathematics, Grade 3

Objective

To add and subtract numbers up to two digits mentally. (This should be taught with the emphasis on the child doing the operation mentally as far as possible.)

Sample Item for Addition

$$
\begin{array}{r}
20 \\
+23 \\
\hline
\end{array}
$$

☐

The number that should be in the box is: (a) 34 (b) 40 (c) 43 (d) 70

Stimulus Attributes

1. First addend should end in zero,
   or
2. The tens should be identical or the units should be identical for the two addends, unless one of the addends is a single-digit number.
3. Set of natural numbers should be given only.
4. Column or horizontal line should appear with the two addends.
5. Sum should be indicated by an empty box.
6. Sum of digits in the unit place position must be less than 10.

Response Attributes

Distracters should target common errors such as:

1. reversal of key (correct answer).
2. addition of digits of one place position only.
3. mistaken choice of operation, such as subtraction instead of addition.

Sample Specifications for Main Idea Comprehension of Written Material, Grade 5

Test items may ask students to:

1. create or choose the most accurate summary of the selection or part of the selection to identify or state the topic of all or a part of the selection,

   or

2. identify or state main idea or central point of a selection or part of that selection,

   or

3. condense explicit information,

   or

4. paraphrase or restate points.

but students should *not* have to make an inference in order to select or construct the appropriate answer. Items can be phrased in a variety of ways, but they *all* must require the student to have recognized the central message or overall point of the selection (or designated part of the selection).

Sample Items (The items could be multiple choice, short answer, or essay.)

Students would be given a reading passage and asked to indicate the central message of the passage or parts of the passage in one of the following ways:

■ What is this selection mainly about?

■ Write a brief paragraph summarizing this passage.

■ Which of these options best summarizes the article?

■ Describe, in one sentence, the passage's central message.

■ What is the main point of this passage?

■ What is the main idea of the passage's fourth paragraph?

From *Tests That Help Teaching*, by W.J. Popham, 1995, Los Angeles, CA: IOX Assessment Associates. Reprinted by permission.

Sample Specification for Interpretive Reading, Grade 6

This specification is a general description that provides a variety of ways that interpretive reading could be measured, thereby encouraging teachers to teach this important skill in several ways.

General Description

The student will analyze characters, infer setting, summarize plot, understand dialogue, sense mood, and interpret figurative language. Some of these skills (such as inferring setting and summarizing plot) apply exclusively to literary passages. Items assessing character analysis, dialogue, mood, and figurative language may occur in social science passages.

Sample Item for Sensing Mood

(A sample passage would be provided.)

1. At the beginning of this story, the mood is one of
   a. disappointment and sorrow
   b. curiosity and excitement
   c. fear and suspense
   d. thankfulness and joy

(This also could be measured using open-ended items such as "How did the mood of the story change from the beginning to the end of the story?" or "Compare the mood of this article with the mood in the TV report of the incident.")

From *Reading Framework for California Public Schools: Kindergarten Through Grade 12*, produced by the California State Department of Education, 1980, Sacramento. Adapted by permission.

APPENDIX F

Sample Communications with Teachers

(This sample is from a guide prepared for teachers of adults and describes how they can assess students' thinking, research, and writing skills by having the students complete a project.)

Student Projects

A project will be produced by the learner, in negotiation with the tutor or teacher. The guidelines given below are aimed at giving learners suggestions on how to choose, develop, and complete a project. These guidelines should be discussed with learners. Projects will be marked by the teacher according to the assessment criteria given below.

What is a project? A project is a piece of written work on a topic of interest to the learner. It can include information that the learner has had to go and get from somewhere or ideas and descriptions that come from a learner's own memories and experiences. A project that is interesting to the reader will usually include some supporting material such as pictures, tables, etc. The main features of a project are as follows:

- A project is a written presentation on a topic based on any of the following: interests, activities, or experience.

- It is made up of a mix of text types and supporting material in a text of minimum 1000 words, maximum 2000 words.

Types of Project Topics

- Interest—this could be something a student reads about or finds out about without being actively involved, such as a hobby, sport, community issue, something of interest at work, etc.

- Activity—this usually refers to something a student is doing now or has been actively involved in, such as building something, sewing, studying, work issues (e.g., a training course taken at work), parenting, leisure activity, formal/informal employment, etc.

- Experience—this is something that reflects on the past, such as personal/family history, community history, memorable or traumatic experience, past work experience, etc.

Anything that a student is interested in and that extends the present knowledge of that student could make a worthwhile project. Based on the categories given above, an interest in any of the following could be developed into a project.

Examples of Project Topics

Finding out more about a favorite football team and its players, an investigation into clothing fashions, running a small business, analyzing how a newspaper balances various aspects (such as politics, sport, and advertising), moving house, marriage, the birth of a baby, township violence, documenting a community issue or activity, surveying opinions on community issues, memories of schooling and of teachers, a visit to some famous place, reviews of a favorite film or TV program, biographies of famous or admired people, and so forth.

Guidelines

These guidelines are to help you guide your learners in their project work. They are directed to learners and should be shared and discussed with them. The guidelines outline the kinds of processes and activities learners should engage in to decide on, develop, and complete a project. They reflect general procedures for all topics.

There are a few points to remember when using these guidelines with your learners. First, these suggestions do not have to be followed in the strict order in which they are laid out. The guidelines work in a cycle, with many of the activities going on at the same time rather than one after the other. For example, a learner might prefer to make a rough draft of headings first in order to decide what kind of information he or she needs to find out.

Second, not all the guidelines have to be followed for every project. A lot will depend on what kind of topic a learner has chosen, and how he or she wants to approach it. For example, someone who chooses to write about something happening at work may not need to research a subject, but may need to d） some simple interviewing with fellow workers.

The main point to bear in mind about the project is that it is a very useful learning tool. Producing a project brings together a lot of

skills that adult learners need in order to pursue their studies: it involves making their own decisions on learning issues, taking control of their own learning, following through on an overall plan, finding out information, and using different kinds of material and information for different purposes.

Many adult learners at this level may be nervous of the idea of a project. Talking about how useful the kinds of learning and organizing skills put forward in the guidelines are and discussing how they can be used in quite simple ways at this level could help lessen these fears.

The project helps us assess learners' information gathering and accessing skills, information processing skills, and information presentation skills. It also helps us promote learners' independent learning, study skills, and integration of their own experience and interest into study.

These guidelines are suggestions for what you as a teacher might say to your learners in order to help them in their project work.

1. How to get started

   ■ Motivate: explain why you are interested in this topic. Your motivation can later be written into your project.

   ■ Define purpose of project (such as to inform others, for my own interest, to keep a record, to try and get action on some issue).

   ■ Plan approach: how will I do it?

2. Next steps

   A. Gathering and recording information (from outside sources and from own experience)

Possible routes:

- reading (research books, magazines)
- interviewing (asking people questions)
- group discussions
- observation
- requesting or sending for information
- reflecting and making notes on one's own experience and knowledge
- using simple questionnaires

B. Processing information

- select information
- identify gaps
- put information into a logical order
- summarize
- interpret/explain
- expand using supplementary material (diagrams, pictures, tables, photos, etc.)
- decide on text types
- draw conclusions

C. Presenting information

- drafting (write out in rough)
- layout: decide on structure, sections, headings, numberings, table of contents, pictures, etc.
- editing: structure, tone, accuracy (of language and of information), clarity of ideas, purpose of project
- final presentation and submission

3. Developing learning-how-to-learn skills

In order for learners to get the most out of their project work, it is sometimes useful for them to think about the processes they have been through once the work is finished. We would suggest that learners be encouraged to write a personal reflection on their learning experience. This is optional and will not be assessed. It can be structured by questions such as the following:

- What did you learn?
- How did you go about this?
- What do you think of the final product?
- Did you enjoy it?
- What were the problems/difficulties you encountered?
- What would you do differently next time?

Assessment Criteria for the Project

Teachers will mark their learners' projects. The assessment criteria are related to the performance outcomes given for the reading and writing elements in the user guide. A project will be assessed on how well it meets these criteria, and will be awarded a grade of Merit, Credit, or Threshold levels, accordingly.

- Content is relevant to the topic and purpose of the project.
- Content is clearly and appropriately sequenced and organized (e.g., table of contents, headings, and sub-headings,

introductions and conclusions, numberings, columns, labels).

- Language (grammar, punctuation, spelling, and vocabulary) expresses the ideas reasonably clearly.

- The project shows evidence of gathering information from outside sources or from own experience.

- The text type(s) used suit the purpose of the project.

- The project brings in relevant support material (diagrams, drawings, pictures, different text types such as letters).

- The final product shows evidence of development from earlier drafts.

- The project meets the length criteria (minimum 1000 words, maximum 2000 words, or between 5 and 10 pages).

- The project is clearly and attractively presented.

A note on drafts: Learners should submit all drafts with the final product. Evidence of checking and editing a piece of writing is a performance outcome that will be assessed. The project is a piece of work done over a period of time, and we would expect a higher level of language than a candidate might be able to show in a more pressured situation. Teachers can help and guide students through the writing of the project, and evidence of this help will not count against candidates. However, the work should originate from the student. Early and later drafts of the writing will show the development that takes place.

From *Adult Basic Education User's Guide, Communications in English Examinations Syllabus*, produced by the Independent Examinations Board, 1994. Johannesburg, South Africa.

Example of Communicating with Teachers on Reading Assessment

Overview: Reading Assessment

For many years, reading tests were based on lists of basic skill objectives because it was thought that students who could respond correctly to items measuring these skills were comprehending effectively. However, distinctions among many of these skills are unclear, and teaching and testing practices related to these narrow skill designations fail to capture the dynamic nature of the reading process. In 1988, as part of a continuing review of the conceptual bases for statewide reading testing, the 60-member Reading Assessment Advisory Committee [of Pennsylvania] designed a reading test that measured a broad range of comprehension abilities as well as other important elements of the reading process. To do this, they examined reading research results from the past 15 years, investigated the revised reading assessments being used by several other states, and studied the implications of the framework for integrating communication skills across the curriculum. Based on these investigations, the committee recommended a definition of reading for teachers.

Reading is a dynamic process in which the reader interacts with the text to construct meaning. Inherent in constructing meaning is the reader's ability to activate prior knowledge, use reading strategies, and adapt to the reading situation.

This definition of reading as a dynamic, interactive process means that a good reader is no longer defined as one who demonstrates mastery of a series of isolated skills, but rather

as one who can apply reading strategies independently and flexibly in a variety of reading situations. Good reading assessments evaluate students' ability to apply their knowledge, skills, and strategies to reading situations that are representative of those they encounter in their classrooms. Based on this definition of reading, the committee recommended that the state assessment measure four elements of the reading process:

1. prior knowledge about the topic,
2. ability to construct meaning to comprehend text,
3. knowledge and use of appropriate reading strategies, and
4. reading habits and attitudes.

Therefore, the reading assessment is based on current thought about teaching reading as a whole, reflective, literary process. Its purpose is to assess students' progress in transacting meaningfully with text, so it reflects the concepts inherent in the framework for teaching communication skills across the curriculum. It measures broad communications outcomes such as constructing meaning from a variety of texts, responding to information and ideas gained by reading texts from various sources, and analyzing and making critical judgements about what is read. In keeping with the active nature of outcome-based assessment, the committee realized that multiple-choice items were probably not the best means of assessing some of the elements. Although multiple-choice tests can be an efficient and effective means of assessing some concepts and ideas, it also is necessary to present students with the opportunity to create varied, reflective responses. Therefore, beginning in 1993, a combination of multiple-choice and open-ended items will be used. The open-ended items will be of two response types: short response, requiring an answer of one paragraph, and extended response, requiring the reader to write several paragraphs.

The assessment procedures for reading will require students to

- indicate whether they use effective before-, during-, or after-reading strategies;

- answer items that activate and assess prior knowledge about the passage they will be reading;

- read one passage, either narrative or informational;

- answer about 15 multiple-choice items, based on constructing meaning around three reading process levels (explicit, implicit, extended) with an emphasis on thinking skills; and

- respond to reading by writing answers to one short-response, open-ended item and one extended-response, open-ended item.

Measuring the Elements of Reading

Reading Strategies

This element of reading is based on research that suggests that effective readers use various strategies before, during, and after reading to gain meaning from text. Before

reading, students should examine the material to determine its basic nature—the general type of text it represents, the overall content to be expected, and the way the passage is structured. This knowledge enables them to set an appropriate purpose for reading. During reading, it is expected that students will proceed fluently through a passage monitoring their comprehension by revising their predictions, self-questioning, forming mental images, paraphrasing, and clarifying misunderstandings. Beyond keeping track of their comprehension process during reading, effective readers engage in strategies that are intended to compensate for, or fix-up, breakdowns in understanding. These fix-up strategies may include reading ahead, rereading, adjusting rate, and seeking outside help from the teacher, a friend, or a resource, like an encyclopedia or a dictionary. After reading, students can summarize the major ideas or events in a selection and critically evaluate the material along several important dimensions including its quality, accuracy, and literary value.

The first items students will encounter in the reading test are those that ask if they use such strategies. They are told that when people read an article, story, book, or textbook, there are things they can do to make what they are reading easier to understand. The students are then presented with a list of five strategies readers use before, during, or after reading. They are asked to think about what they would do in that situation and then read each statement on the list. If it is a strategy they sometimes or often use, they are directed to mark "Y" for "Yes" on their answer sheet. If they seldom or never use the strategy, they are to mark "N" for "No." School personnel will be able to determine from resulting data which strategies students claim they are using to plan instruction accordingly.

Prior Knowledge

When people encounter new information, they attempt to understand it by fitting it into what they already know about the world. Research has shown that the knowledge and experience a reader brings to the reading process is a critical factor influencing comprehension. Effective readers access or activate their prior knowledge about the central themes, major concepts, or details expected in a passage. They then use this in conjunction with new information from the passage to construct meaning and understand it. Readers who have little or no prior knowledge about a text's topic, or who fail to access what knowledge they do have before reading, have more difficulty understanding it than those who have familiarity with the topic. This is why teachers use many different kinds of prereading and directed reading experiences before assigning an actual reading task and why they teach students to ask questions and make predictions about what they read.

After the five strategy items, students are presented with a set of five (at grade 11) or ten (at grades 5 and 8) questions which they again answer "Yes" or "No." These items focus on topics and concepts central to the understanding of the passages used in the assessment, but they are designed to activate as well as assess prior knowledge, so they are relatively easy for most students. For example, a prior-knowledge item for a passage that is about a city afire may ask if fire could burn more rapidly if the city's houses were mostly made of wood. This is quite an easy item; most students know that wood burns readily.

Constructing Meaning

Encouraged by the ideas set forth by the framework committee for teaching communication skills across the curriculum and by the structure and format of the statewide assessment program in the past three years, teachers are changing the way they teach reading. They are integrating all of the language arts and using content area texts as sources of language instruction material. They are using whole texts, whether trade books or chapters from textbooks, to teach students how to "transact with text"—to use prior knowledge and metacognitive strategies and to respond to literature as well as to construct meaning from it—in order to get the most out of what they read. Teachers are teaching students that there may be more than one right answer to almost any question. They are teaching students how to use thinking skills, such as inference, comparison, and evaluation, to generate several appropriate responses to a task.

As a result of these activities, teachers also should be assessing students' learning in different ways. They should be relying less on standardized, end-of-book and teacher-made multiple-choice tests and more on requiring students to respond to learning in other ways, such as by producing a paper, artwork, play, or speech that can show in depth what they have learned. Students may be building portfolios so that they and their teachers (and parents) can constantly assess their progress.

Some samples of tasks required by open-ended items may be

1. to measure "developing interpretation":
   - summarizing the passage
   - analyzing a character's actions
   - analyzing two points of view from the passage
   - comparing a character's characteristics at the beginning and end of the passage

2. to measure "responding personally":
   - listing previously known information and comparing it with information learned from the passage
   - writing an appropriate or alternate ending to the passage
   - listing legitimate inferences made from the passage and why they are reasonable
   - rewriting the story from another character's point of view
   - explaining agreement or disagreement with the author

3. to measure "responding critically":
   - hypothesizing why an author says something in the passage
   - explaining why a title is or is not appropriate
   - evaluating the author's intentions: detecting bias or other attempts at reader manipulation
   - hypothesizing why an author uses a certain literary technique
   - explaining the author's point of view
   - listing character enhancements developed in the passage and explaining how the author develops them

Each student will respond to 15 multiple-choice items worth one point each, one open-ended item worth three points, and one open-ended item worth five points. Therefore, responding to literature through writing responses to open-ended items will account for about one-third of a school's score.

From the *Reading Assessment Handbook*, produced by the Pennsylvania State Department of Education, Division of Evaluation and Reports, 1992, Harrisburg. Adapted by permission.

REFERENCES

ADVANCING BASIC EDUCATION AND LITERACY. (1993). *Classroom in a suitcase* (A Project ABEL Information Bulletin, #27). Washington, DC: Academy for Educational Development.

AHMED, M., CHABBOTT, C., JOSHI, A., & PANDE, R. (1993). *Primary education for all: Learning from the BRAC experience.* Washington, DC: Project ABEL, Advancing Basic Education and Literacy.

AMERICAN PSYCHOLOGICAL ASSOCIATION. (1985). *Standards for educational and psychological testing.* Washington, DC: Author.

ASMERSON, K., AND OTHERS. (1989). *Discontinuations of students from institutions of higher learning in Ethiopia.* Unpublished document. Addis Ababa: University of Addis Ababa.

BADGER, E. (1995). *The role of expectations and fairness in state wide assessment programs: Lessons from Massachusetts.* Boston, MA: Massachusetts State Department of Education.

BAKER, E.L., ASCHBACHER, P., NIEMI, D., & SATO, E. (1992). *CRESST performance assessment models: Assessing content area explanations* (CSE Technical Report Series). Los Angeles, CA: National Center for Research on Evaluation, Standards, and Student Testing.

BAKER, E.L., O'NEIL, H.F., & LINN, R.L. (1993, December). Policy and validity prospects for performance-based assessment. *American Psychologist,* 1210–1218.

BARON, J.B. (ED.). (1993). *Assessment as an opportunity to learn: The Connecticut common core of learning alternative assessment of secondary school science and mathematics.* Hartford, CT: Connecticut State Department of Education.

BARON, J.B., FORGIONE, P.D., RINDONE, D.A., KRUGLANSKI, H., & DAVEY, B. (1989, April). *Toward a new generation of student outcome measures: Connecticut's common core of learning assessment.* Paper presented at the annual meeting of the American Educational Research Association, San Francisco, CA.

BLALOCK, H.M. (1968). The measurement problem. In H.M. Blalock & A. Blalock (Eds.), *Methodology in social research.* New York: McGraw-Hill.

BLOOM, B.S. (ED.). (1956). *Taxonomy of educational objectives: The classification of educational goals, Handbook 1: Cognitive domain.* New York: McKay.

BRIDGEMAN, B., & WENDLER, C. (1989). *Prediction of grades in college mathematics courses as a component of the placement validity of SAT-mathematics scores.* New York: College Board.

CALIFORNIA STATE DEPARTMENT OF EDUCATION. (1979a). *Proficiency assessment handbook.* Sacramento, CA: Author.

CALIFORNIA STATE DEPARTMENT OF EDUCATION. (1979b). *Proficiency assessment handbook: Bias and fairness in proficiency assessment* (Appendix M). Sacramento, CA: Author.

CALIFORNIA STATE DEPARTMENT OF EDUCATION. (1980). *Reading framework for California public schools: Kindergarten through grade 12.* Sacramento, CA: Author.

CALIFORNIA STATE DEPARTMENT OF EDUCATION. (1989a). *A question of thinking: A first look at students' performance on open-ended questions in mathematics* (California Assessment Program). Sacramento, CA: Author.

CALIFORNIA STATE DEPARTMENT OF EDUCATION. (1989b). *Survey of academic skills: Grade 8, 1989.* (California Assessment Program). Sacramento, CA: Author.

CALIFORNIA STATE DEPARTMENT OF EDUCATION. (1990a). *New directions in science assessment* (California Assessment Program). Sacramento, CA: Author.

CALIFORNIA STATE DEPARTMENT OF EDUCATION. (1990b). *Survey of academic skills: Writing achievement, grade 12, 1989–90* (California Assessment Program). Sacramento, CA: Author.

CALIFORNIA STATE DEPARTMENT OF EDUCATION. (1990c). *Writing assessment handbook*. (California Assessment Program). Sacramento, CA: Author.

CALIFORNIA STATE DEPARTMENT OF EDUCATION. (1991a). *A sampler of mathematics assessment* (California Assessment Program). Sacramento, CA: Author.

CALIFORNIA STATE DEPARTMENT OF EDUCATION. (1991b). *California assessment program field test collection: Working materials*. Sacramento, CA: Author.

CALIFORNIA STATE DEPARTMENT OF EDUCATION. (1991c). *Preliminary edition. Survey of academic skills—science* (California Assessment Program). Sacramento, CA: Author.

CALIFORNIA STATE DEPARTMENT OF EDUCATION. (1992). *A sampler of English-language arts assessment: Elementary, preliminary edition* (California Assessment Program). Sacramento, CA: Author.

CAPPER, J. (1994). *CRT review and assessment*. Unpublished report to USAID/Ghana.

CHOPPIN, B.H. (1990). Prediction of success in higher education. In H.J. Walberg & G.D. Haertel (Eds.), *The international encyclopedia of educational evaluation*. New York: Pergamon.

CLEARY, T.A., & HILTON, T.L. (1968). An investigation into item bias. *Educational and Psychological Measurement, 8*, 61–75.

DENVIR, B., & BROWN, M. (1986). Understanding of number concepts in low-attaining 7–9 year olds: Part II, the teaching studies. *Educational Studies in Mathematics, 17*, 143–164.

EISEMON, T.O. (1990). Examinations policies to strengthen primary schooling in African countries. *International Journal of Educational Development, 10*(1), 68–82.

EVANS, H. (1988). *Strengthening of secondary education* (General curriculum: A study of five parishes). Final Report to the UNDP. Kingston, Jamaica: World Bank.

Fairness in standardized tests: Oversight Hearings before the Subcommittee on Civil and Constitutional Rights, U.S. Congress, 100th Cong., 1st Sess. (1987) (testimony of P. Rosser).

GIPPS, C. (1990). *National curriculum assessment: A research agenda*.

GREANEY, V., & KELLAGHAN, T. (1995). *Equity issues in public examinations in developing countries*. (World Bank Technical Paper No. 272; Asia Technical Series). Washington, DC: World Bank.

HERMAN, J., ASCHBACHER, P., & WINTERS, L. (1992). *A practical guide to alternative assessment*. Alexandria, VA: Association for Supervision and Curriculum Development.

INDEPENDENT EXAMINATIONS BOARD. (1994). *Adult basic education user's guide, communications in English examinations syllabus*. Johannesburg, South Africa.

INDEPENDENT EXAMINATIONS BOARD. (1994). *The mathematics assessment package* (Adult Basic Education, level 3, user guide 2). Johannesburg, South Africa: Author.

KELLAGHAN, T. (1993, January). *Can public examinations be used to provide information for national assessment?* Paper prepared for a Seminar on National Assessment Systems for Africa, Nairobi.

KELLAGHAN, T., & GREANEY, V. (1992). *Using examinations to improve education: A study in fourteen African countries*. Washington, DC: World Bank.

KELLY, M.J. (1986). *An overview of education in Zambia*. Lusaka: University of Zambia.

KENYA NATIONAL EXAMINATIONS COUNCIL. (1980). *Kenya Certificate of Primary Education Newsletter*. Nairobi: Author.

KENYA NATIONAL EXAMINATIONS COUNCIL. (1981). *Kenya Certificate of Primary Education Newsletter*. Nairobi: Author.

MASSACHUSETTS STATE DEPARTMENT OF EDUCATION. (1990). *Using the school report*. Boston, MA: Author.

MAYER, R. (1989). Models for understanding. *Review of Educational Research, 59*(1), 43–64.

MCCLENAN, V., & MORGAN, H. (1989). *First steps in science, pupil's book 6*. Kingston, Jamaica: Longman.

MCCLENAN, V., POTTINGER, D., & GORDON, M. (1990). *First steps in science, pupil's book 4*. Kingston, Jamaica: Longman.

NAMIBIA MINISTRY OF EDUCATION AND CULTURE. (1994). *Social studies pilot programme: Continuous assessment 1*. Windhoek, Namibia: Ministry of

Education and Culture, Centre for Applied Social Sciences.

NAMIBIA MINISTRY OF EDUCATION AND CULTURE. (1995). *Teacher's guide to the syllabus* (Natural science and health education, grade five). Windhoek, Namibia: Author.

NITKO, A.J. (1996). *Educational assessment of students* (2nd ed.). Columbus, OH: Merrill.

NUMMELA, R.M., & ROSENGREN, T.M. (1986). The triune brain: A new paradigm for education. *Journal of Humanistic Education and Development, 24,* 98–102.

OLOO, A. (1990, February 3). KCPE ranking is wrong. *Daily Nation,* Nairobi.

PENNSYLVANIA STATE DEPARTMENT OF EDUCATION. DIVISION OF EVALUATION AND REPORTS. (1992). *Reading assessment handbook.* Harrisburg, PA: Author.

PENNSYLVANIA STATE DEPARTMENT OF EDUCATION, DIVISION OF EVALUATION AND REPORTS. (1992). *Writing assessment handbook.* Harrisburg, PA: Author.

POLYA, G. (1973). *Instruction and analogy in mathematics.* Princeton, NJ: Princeton University Press.

POPHAM, W.J., (1995). *Tests that help teaching.* Los Angeles, CA: IOX Assessment Associates.

PRAWAT, R.S. (1989). Promoting access to knowledge, strategy, and disposition in students: A research synthesis. *Review of Educational Research, 59*(1), 1–41.

PUNJAB. (1992). *Commission for evaluation of examination system and eradication of malpractices.* Report. Lahore: Author.

PURYEAR, J.M. (1993). *Status and problem of international education statistics and research.* Paper presented at a meeting of the Board on International Comparative Studies in Education, National Academy of Sciences, Washington, DC.

RESNICK, L. (1987). *Education and learning to think.* Washington, DC: National Academy Press.

ROSSER, P. (1989). *The SAT gender gap.* Washington, DC: Center for Women's Policy Studies.

ROWELL, P., & PROPHET, R. (1990). Curriculum-in-action: The "practical" dimension in Botswana classrooms. *International Journal of Educational Development, 10*(1), 17–26.

SELKOW, P. (1984). *Assessing sex bias in testing.* New York: Greenwood.

SMITH, M.L. (1991, June/July). Put to the test: The effects of external testing on teachers. *Educational Researcher,* 8–11.

SOMERSET, H.C.A. (1965). *Untitled report.* Nairobi, Kenya: East African Publishing House.

SOMERSET, H.C.A. (1993). *Examinations and the quality of education.* Unpublished paper. Washington, DC: World Bank.

STIGLER, J.W., & PERRY, M. (1987). Cross-cultural studies of mathematics teaching and learning: Recent findings and new directions. *Effective Mathematics Teaching,* 194–223.

SWAZILAND MINISTRY OF EDUCATION. (1992). *National curriculum centre/continuous assessment unit, EPMT project.* Mbabane, Swaziland: Author.

TEXAS EDUCATION AGENCY. (1995). *Texas assessment of academic skills: 1990–1995 science objectives and measurement specifications tested at grade 8.* Austin, TX: Author.

TORRANCE, H. (1993). Combining measurement-driven instruction with authentic assessment: Some initial observations of national assessment in England and Wales. *Educational Evaluation and Policy Analysis, 15*(1), 81–90.

TRAVERS, K.J. ET AL. (1985). *Second international mathematics study summary report for the United States.* Champaign, IL: Stipes.

WAINER, H., & STEINBERG, L. (1990). *Sex differences in performance on the mathematics section of the scholastic aptitude test: A bidirectional validity study.* Princeton, NJ: Educational Testing Service.

WEN, B. (1993). An analysis of the decline in the scores of the college-university entrance examination in Beijing Municipality. *Chinese Education and Society, 26,* 47–58.

WENDLER, C., & CARLTON, S. (1987, April). *An examination of SAT verbal items for differential performance by women and men: An exploratory study.* Paper presented at the annual meeting of the American Educational Research Association, Washington, DC.

WINERIP, M. (1994, February 16). Merit scholarship program faces sex bias complaint. *New York Times.*

WOLF, D.P., & REARDON, S.F. (1993, March 11–12). *Equity in the design of performance assessments: A handle to wind up the tongue with?* Paper prepared for presentation at the Ford Foundation Symposium on Equity and Educational Testing and Assessment, Washington, DC.

AUTHOR INDEX

Note: An "f" following an index entry indicates that the citation may be found in a figure, a "t" that it may be found in a table, and an "n" that it may be found in a note.

SUBJECT INDEX

Note: An "f" following an index entry indicates that the citation may be found in a figure, a "t" that it may be found in a table, and an "n" that it may be found in a note.

SCIENTIFIC METHOD: sample item specifications, 172–174

SCORE: definition of, vii

SCORING: passing scores, 43. *see also* Grading; Marking

SCORING GUIDES: analytic, 170–171; for group participation, 34, 35f–36f; holistic, 168–169

SECONDARY-LEVEL SCIENCE: thematic multiple-choice questions for, 62f–63f, 62–64

SELECTION EXAMINATIONS, 28–30; gender bias in, 135–137

SHORT-ANSWER ITEMS, 61

SKILLS: number of items tested per, 42–43; partial matrix for, 89, 91f–93f; prompting students to use, 68; reading area, 89, 90f, 91f–93f

SPEAKING TASKS: checklist for grading, 164–167

SPECIFICATIONS: to communicate with teachers and educators, 106–107; essay test, 71, 72f, 73f, 74f; as guides for item writers, 97–98; importance of, 96–99; and item bank preparations, 98–99; test item, 96–109, 102f–103f, 104f, 105f, 172–178; and test validity, 96–97; and what is important to learn, 99; writing, 101–106

STAFF DEVELOPMENT: marking as, 77

STANDARD: definition of, vii

STANDARDS, MULTIPLE: inequities due to, 139

STORY WRITING, 66

STUDENT CHOICE: in examinations, 82–83

STUDENT CRITIQUE OF PROFICIENCY TESTS, 134–135; sample form for, 136f

STUDENT PROJECTS, 179; assessment criteria for, 181–182; guidelines for, 180–181

STUDENTS: comparison of, 84; examination takers, 84–85; specifications and, 99

SUBGROUPS: identifying biased items in subtests with, 135, 137t, 138t

SUBJECTS: areas tested, 82; covering in depth, 8–11; student choice in, 82–83

SUBTESTS: identifying biased items in, 135, 137t, 138t

SUDAN: gender balance in, 133

SUFFICIENT-ITEM RELIABILITY, 42

SUPERMARKET PRICES: comparing, 151–154

T

TANZANIA: gender balance in, 133

TASKS: performance, 46–60, 62; real-life, 22

TEACHER RESISTANCE: avoiding, 128–130; strategies to reduce, 129–130

TEACHERS: benefits of involving, 37; California's Report of Writing Achievement, 115, 117f–118f; classroom assessment for, 142–147; how to communicate with, 107, 108f; Kenya's Report, 115, 116f; marking as staff development for, 77; marking essay tests, 66–67; marking tips for, 161–163; reports for, 115–119; sample communications with, 179–186; specifications and, 99; specifications to communicate with, 106–107

THINKING, HIGHER, 5–8; test questions that promote, 6–8, 7f
TOGO: national assessment in, 83
TOPICS: covering in depth, 8–11
TRAINING MARKERS, 77–78
TRANSFERABILITY, 22

U

UNITED KINGDOM: national assessment system, 44n; teacher resistance in, 128, 129
UNITED STATES: gender bias in, 134, 135; national assessment system, 44n
URBAN SCHOOLS: test report comparing, 121, 122f

V

VALIDITY, 37–38, 38–40, 40–41; content, 39; criteria for, 40–41; curricular and instructional, 39–40; definition of, viii; determining, 38–39; of essay tests, 70–78; how to ensure, 42–43; need to ensure, 42; predictive, 40; specifications and, 96–97

W

WORLD BANK, 83
WRITERS, ITEM: specifications as guides for, 97–98
WRITING: autobiographical, 65; integrating with reading, 67–68; observational, 66; performance tasks, 47–50, 48f–50f, 51–52; story, 66; teaching, 65–66; types of, 65–66. *see also* Essays; Reading
WRITING ASSESSMENT: how to communicate with teachers about, 107, 108f
WRITING COMPREHENSION: sample specification for, 177
WRITING INSTRUCTION: testing to improve, 65–68
WRITING PROMPTS, 68, 71–73; history, 155; sample, 75f, 163
WRITING SPECIFICATIONS: sample, 177; and weaknesses in curriculum and textbooks, 106; who should be involved in, 101–106
WRITING TESTS, 65–66; history, 159–160; research on, 68–70

Z

ZIMBABWE: gender balance in, 133